The Romancer

Memory is the way we keep telling ourselves - and other people – a somewhat different version of our stories. We can hardly tell our lives without an ongoing narrative.

Alice Munro

Novels by Wendy Robertson

Theft
Lizza
The Real Life of Studs McGuire
French Leave
Riches of The Earth
Under a Brighter Sky
Land of Your Possession
A Dark Light Shining
Kitty Rainbow
Cruelty Games
Children of the Storm
A Thirsting Land
The Jagged Window
My Dark Eyed Girl
Self Made Woman
Where Hope Lives
Long Journey Home
Honesty's Daughter
A Woman Scorned
No Rest For the Wicked
Family Ties
The Lavender House
Sandie Shaw and the Millionth Marvell Cooker
The Woman Who Drew Buildings
An Englishwoman in France
The Art of Retreating

Obtainable from *www.headline.co.uk*
or *www.severnhouse.com*

Or direct from Wendy Robertson at
www.wendyrobertson.com

The Romancer

On Being a Writer

Wendy Robertson

Room
To
Write

www.roomtowrite.co.uk

Published by Room To Write

www.roomtowrite.co.uk

ISBN 978-0-9564823-3-4

Designed and produced by **hpm**group. Tel 0191 3006941
www.hpm.uk.com

Cover image by Fiona Naughton
www.fionanaughtonartworks.com

For Barbara, Billy, Tom, Susan & Ian,
Bryan, Debora, Grahame & Angus
– then and now –
always an inspiration

And with heartfelt thanks to my friends, writers Gillian
Wales and Avril Joy, who inspired *The Romancer*
and gave graceful support in the writing of it.
And thank you to Fiona Naughton for allowing me
to use her fine portait for the cover.
And more special thanks to John Alderson and Steve Tolson
who make very good books.

Contents

Setting the Scene

I am a lifelong admirer of the art of the biographer, who lives in the halfway house between history and personality. Returning from lunch with biographer Kathleen Jones one day, my head full of her new work on Katherine Mansfield and its connections with her biography of Catherine Cookson, I was suddenly inspired to make a 'valid connection' between my own life and my writing: a kind of creative memoir.

So I embarked on *The Romancer* - not a conventional memoir, but a kaleidoscope with all the elements of my life and experience as glittering fragments in the drum. Every time I shake this kaleidoscope a complex pattern emerges: each new pattern is a novel or story unique in itself.

The Romancer is made up of three parts. First comes *Inspirations,* an account of elements - people, experiences, places, insights and feelings - from my own life that have, whether or not I was conscious of it, inspired my wide range of novels and stories. Inevitably this is the largest part of this book. Without such inspirations would there be anything to write? These elements are the glittering fragments in the drum of the kaleidoscope.

Then *Onto The Page* celebrates many things - the poetic charm of getting the right words in the right place, the development of character, the evocation of place, the organisation of ideas, the architectural skills of building a novel and the joys of editing and shaping one's own prose. It involves seeing one's work into print and the surreal, occasionally comical, vagaries of the world of publication.

My great wish is that both readers and writers will relish *The Romancer*; that it may unlock for them some secrets of the art of fiction and influence their appreciation of the novel in general. I hope also that writers in particular will be inspired through these pages to write on, and acquire some strategies and skills to enhance their own writing experience.

Only in retrospect - in writing *The Romancer* - have I finally made some crucial connections myself, recognising now how all that stuff buried deep in my subconscious has turned up on the page. I have become more aware of the novelist's role as an historian of private lives, shaking and shaking the kaleidoscope and coming up with stories that have universal appeal.

Of course we have to remember that *The Romancer* itself is a kind of fiction – a narrative of narratives, a story of stories.

Wendy Robertson

Inspirations

Dreamer

They called me dreamer when I was small. There's a photo of me sitting on my mother's knee, a deep frown on my round brow. When I was older strangers in the street would call after me, 'Don't worry, pet. It might never happen.'

There has always been this space in my head where I retreat to think and worry about my world and to weave new worlds, invent new people, new narratives that make sense of the astonishing things that I see, hear and feel.

This place is not always a happy place as it contains everything - the dark as well as the light. Experiencing life in this way means you remember everything. Always. My sister doesn't remember everything; the dark things have faded for her, which is a good thing.

One way to recognise these experiences, to bring them outside that interior space, is to *write* them – more particularly to make stories from them: a rounded narrative is a blessing of expression, containment, and control. But even so, my many novels and stories are not really *about* me - in fact their pages harbour more brightness than shade. Paradoxically the dark elements lodged inside this interior space can generate shards of light that bring characters to life, illuminate events, excavate experiences and induce sensual recall.

The habit of story-making is, I think, a neat balance between nature and nurture. My father wrote tender philosophical letters; my mother made stories of everything, including history and politics. What she didn't know, she made up. Once, when she was young, she was called to her head-teacher's room to explain her use of the word *zephyr* in a poem, and was accused of plagiarizing it. She hadn't.

On the nurture side, I would listen as she and her sisters told and retold stories of their own lives, of the lives of their formidable mother and their dead soldier-father. Listening to these women was how I learned of the close relationship between hard fact and flexible fiction. They would exchange and embellish stories. For instance, there was the *Milk Can Story*. Each day one unlucky member in the family had to take a wire handled can to collect milk from the farm on the corner of their long street. One game, on the way back from the farm, was to swing the can round and round over your head. You had to do it very quickly or the lid of the can would come off. It was my mother Barbara's turn. This day the young Barbara tried swinging it for the first time. The inevitable happened. The milk was spilt and her nice cardigan was drenched. 'My mother,' she would conclude thoughtfully, 'she nearly killed us.'

I came to hear her sisters tell the story as though it had happened to *them*. It would always end with the reference to their mother *nearly killing* them. I still don't know which sister it really happened to. And here I am retelling the tale. Is this fiction or fact?

I think Barbara herself was a dreamer. In a very active, hardworking family, dominated by her Wesleyan mother Sarah Ellen, Sundays were strictly kept as a day of rest: no playing, working or *doing* - just Sunday School and the Bible and singing hymns at the harmonium played by Sarah Ellen. But Barbara as a small child had rheumatic fever and was left with what was known as St Vitus' Dance, the fidgeting disease. The doctor had told Sarah Ellen that her daughter must be allowed to be active, even on Sundays. So, on Sundays, Barbara was allowed to read her books, sitting under the long tablecloth that covered the Singer Sewing Machine, so the sight of her enjoyment did not disturb her brothers' and sisters' still Sunday virtue.

At least that's the story I heard.

My second children's story *Lizza* sprang from my mother's own story. At the age of fourteen, having been sacked from domestic work for acting *above herself*, she was sent off by her mother Sarah Ellen to Bradford to work in the mills. For many years she would say to me, 'I could never understand why my mother sent me there. I could have *gone wrong* you know.'

Going wrong, of course, was the euphemism for getting pregnant.

She didn't get pregnant but she did forge an independent soul that set her outside the world of her siblings for much of the rest of her life. She became a nurse. She lived a good deal of time away from the sacred North East hearth, until the death of her husband Billy, my father - when she came 'home' and was never really happy again.

The mantra *I don't know why my mother sent me* echoed in my ears as I grew up, got married and had my own children. Then, when my own daughter was fourteen years old, my mother told us the story yet again. I looked at them, from the girl to the woman and I finally understood. They were alike, slightly fey, intelligent, articulate: prepared to stand their ground. Barbara was strong and would survive. I could see that would have been Sarah Ellen's judgment. And I know she would have said going to Bradford was for Barbara's *own good*.

So I wrote *Lizza*, the story of the girl who was sent away to Bradford to work in the mills and might have *gone wrong*. I didn't ask my mother any more about her experiences: apart from the *sending away* I invented everything else, as writers do. I set it against the dramas of the 1926 miners' strike and focused on what might have happened to a fey, intelligent, tough little girl, in her view rejected by her mother and left in that wild mill town to fend for herself.

The novel must have had some quality because Hodder and Stoughton accepted it. It was sent by me to them out of the blue - randomly chosen as I had no agent, adviser or useful contact. They accepted it straight away and it remained popular in libraries for many years.

My mother Barbara never saw *Lizza* in published form but she did see it in printers' proofs. I left the proofs with her overnight to read and returned the next day in some trepidation. (She was, in her own way, no less formidable than Sarah Ellen). If she'd hated it I didn't know what I would have done. My precious original work would be blown out of the water.

I called on her on my way home from work. She made me my usual cup of tea and we sat on opposites sides of the table. The stack of printers' proofs sat on the table between us like a pile of unpaid bills. 'Well, pet,' she said, 'I couldn't put it down! Stayed up until two o'clock this morning to get it finished …'

I waited for the 'but…'

'You know the foreman at the factory? You called him Mr Singer. Well his real name was Ernest Smith and you just got him right. And you got the factory right. And the bobbins… and that girl…'

I breathed out and reflected on the trance-like magic of the writing process. This event taught me so much about writing fiction. Barbara had joined in with my take on her world. She'd told me none of those things – not about Ernest Smith, the bobbins, the girl. Yet they were all right to her. Truth and fiction, like two hands clasping, had produced a greater truth, like a magician creating a white dove that could fly free in the air.

Barbara never saw *Lizza* between covers. I've never regretted so much the long hiaitus between acceptance and publication.

From *Lizza* *(1987)* Lizza's older sister Ivy takes her into the mill for the first time:

> …Ivy led Lizza through the big door to a glassed-off office in the corner of the delivery bay. She knocked on the door and responded to the roar from inside by pushing it open. The tiny office was all desk and chair…The man sitting at the desk was small and grey haired, narrow faced like a whippet… His skin was brown, as though he'd been in the sun for many months. Lizza could smell old sweat and warm wool.
>
> Ivy lifted her arm and put her hand on the door jamb. Lizza was aware again of the slim outline of her sister's body. 'Now Mr Singer,' said Ivy, 'I got me sister here. Can you remember me telling you?'
>
> He stood up, pushing his glasses up on the bridge of his nose. 'She looks young, Ivy.'
>
> 'I'm fourteen,' said Lizza.
>
> 'Have you worked before?'
>
> 'Yes, I have.'
>
> 'Where? In a factory?'

'No. A shop. And then in somebody's house.'

'Mills aren't like that, love. Hard places, mills. Don't think she'd do, Ivy. Too fresh. They'd eat her for breakfast, that lot in there.'

'She'll be all right, Mr Singer. 'They're tough where we come from. Isn't all down to looks, you know.'

Lizza spoke up. 'I can do anything you ask. Anything. And I don't let anybody eat me up. Not me.' …

Writer

I felt I could write before I could read or write.

Picture this. A little girl of three in a Fair Isle cardigan, playing outside a house in Lancaster. With her head of Shirley Temple curls she's winsome, prettier than she'll ever be in the many years to come. She's chalking on the sill of the big bay window.

She stands back. That looks right. Just like she has seen her mother do, when she writes her letters. But then the little girl frowns her characteristic frown. Are the squiggles all in one or are there breaks in the line? She runs inside and climbs up to the mantelpiece where she knows there are letters.

Letters are big in her house these days. There are letters from her Daddy who's making aero engines in another city. Mammy reads these out to them all, the four of them sitting round the table. The letters always end with *Love, Bill*. The little girl likes the way her mother smiles as she reads them. But there was one letter that made her mother cry, about someone called Jimmy, whose plane crashed in America. There's a photo of Jimmy in uniform on the mantelpiece, a sharp face with smiling eyes under a peaked cap.

Now, the little girl takes one of her Daddy's letters and looks at it carefully. Ah, yes! There are gaps between the squiggles. So she goes outside and - with the corner of her cardigan – knitted by her Auntie Louie who once told her a tale of swinging a milk can – the little girl rubs the sill so there are now spaces and it is *real* writing.

Smiler

When we were young my younger brother's nickname was Smiler. This was not because he grinned all the time, but because whenever he was emotional, embarrassed or under pressure he would smile. As the third and fourth children in a pressured household the two of us were left to our own devices a good deal. In those days we were quite close. I felt protective towards him and I worried about him, because he could be sparky and mischievous. He was only five when our father died and I've since thought that - unlike the rest of us – his habit was to look forwards rather than backwards. So he always seemed more carefree and optimistic.

My mother Barbara always declared that she had *no* favourites but it was as clear as a red London bus that she loved most - and even indulged - the boy they called Smiler. She called him her *ewe lamb*. Perhaps his free spirit brought some light into her life, making the darkness around her recede.

My brother was always off on his own or with a mate and one night he came into the house hefting a heavy cardboard box. Barbara was out of the house. She was working on the Tote at the local dog track, where she put in two nights a week to supplement her factory wages. The hospital shift system meant that, as a single parent of four children, she couldn't use her training and vocation as a psychiatric nurse. She found the working at the factory hard, feeling out of place. But she worked both there and at the dog track to earn money to keep us all going. That was one of many sacrifices she made which, even then, I knew she was making.

(Oh! I even worked at the dog track myself as a teenager, selling programmes and taking the names for the dogs racing the next week; all pennies to the communal pot. I once wrote a children's novel about children playing around a dog track but never got to finish it.)

Anyway, this night, my brother tips out the contents of the box and onto the table fall books of all kinds - novels, dictionaries, fact books. He's watching me for my reaction. He knows I love books and I already own a own small collection, culled from jumble sales.

'What ya think?' he says, grinning.

This important remembered event is at the core of my very first novel *Theft*, published by Corgi Carousel in 1972. I own two precious copies of this novel – probably the only two copies in the world.

From the children's story ***Theft*** *(1972):*

> 'Well, where did you get them?'
>
> We'd settled down in our beds, on either side of the narrow room, and had waited for the familiar sound of heavy breathing from the other side of the wooden partition. Mam was asleep.
>
> 'It doesn't really matter, does it?' Teddy's voice was muffled by the bedclothes. We always pulled them right up to our ears to keep out the cold of the room.
>
> 'I just want to know.' I said.
>
> 'I found them on that wasteland behind the gasworks. There was one of those tramp-marks on the ground, so I dug down and there they were.'
>
> 'Daft! Don't believe you. Those books have never been underground.'
>
> 'Well, OK. I went down the street, and down that pub behind Woolworths. Called *The Grapes*. You know. Porky said he knew a way in. Round the back.'
>
> 'Porky!' I said, in disgust.
>
> 'I don't know what you're bothered about him for. He's all right, is Porky. Anyway we climbed over the fence

into the back yard. Lots of sheds and barrels and things. So we had a scrounge around. The books were in a big tin trunk.'

'Was it all right to bring them?'

'Yeah. Course it was. They wouldn't have been pushed out into that old shed to rot, if the people wanted them, would they?'

I put my hand under the bed and felt the cardboard box, now stuffed with the precious books. Still there. I turned over and pulled the blanket over my head. Maybe it wasn't right to take them, but who would know, anyway?

The next day Porky called for Teddy before we got up, so he had to sit in the kitchen and wait while Teddy got himself a sandwich. It was after ten o'clock but we never bothered about getting up early during the holidays. Mam always got herself out to the factory at seven o'clock without waking us.

I was making myself a sandwich when Porky actually spoke to me. 'How old are *you*, then?'

'Ten, Nearly.'

'Did you like the books we got you?' He was looking at me quite kindly. I was just wishing he'd pretend again I wasn't there.

'Yes, they're smashing,' I said, biting hard on my sandwich. 'A bit old, though.'

'So what're you gunna do with them?'

'Read them, I suppose.' I chewed the sandwich and there was silence. 'I might start a library...' As soon as I said that I could have bitten off my tongue. This was an idea I'd had for a long time.

I saw the boys grinning at each other and my face was hot.

When they had gone, I dashed upstairs and brought down the cardboard box of books. I spread them out on the hearthrug so I could have a good look at every one. I lit the gas fire to dry them out and began to read the one with the most pictures. I spent the rest of the day reading them and turning over the pages. Just before teatime; just before my Mam got home, I made some paste out of flour and water and stuck clean pages from an old diary in the front of each book. That would do for the date, although I would have to write it with pencil as I didn't have a date-stamp...

Theft is a morality tale: a battle between notions of property and theft. Most importantly it is something of an adventure, as May and Teddy, in trying to right their own wrong, come across real thieves about their regular business.

How *Theft* came to be published is a story in itself. At that time I was at home with two small children. I loved this interlude, letting the dust build up somewhat and writing when they were asleep. That was when I wrote *Theft*. It seemed a time of such freedom.

At that time I was a member of an association called *The Federation of Children's Book Groups,* which aimed to get more books into the hands of more children. It was lead by a very charismatic young woman called Anne Wood who lived in London but came from my home town and had been to my grammar school, although I'd never met her. One day she came north to visit her father and we had a little meeting with other like-minded people in my house. Towards the end of the meeting I mentioned that I'd just finished writing this story called *Theft*. She asked if she could read it. I handed it to her, apologizing for the rather scruffy copy, as this was my only one. I was delighted that anyone at all would take the trouble to read this, my first full length novel.

The next morning she rang me to tell me she liked it. I was so pleased about this, as Anne had turned out to be so informed, so savvy in the field of children's fiction. Then she continued. 'So I think we'll take it.'

'*We?*' I was puzzled.

'Corgi Carousel. That's *Transworld Publishing*.' She went on to tell me that she'd just been appointed the first editor for Transworld's new children's imprint and had the power, there and then, to say 'Yes.'

And she said yes. How magical was that?

Even more interesting than that, *this* was the Anne Wood who went on to set up the independent TV production company, *Ragdoll,* which produced, among other excellent programmes, *Rosie and Jim*, *Tots TV*, *Teletubbies*, and *In the Night Garden*. *This* was the Anne Wood who was to be listed as the third richest person in British broadcasting in 2001, with the value of her business estimated by Broadcast magazine to be £130m. Her charity, The Ragdoll Foundation, went on to lead the field in imaginative philanthropy aimed towards children.

I met Anne when she was on the cusp of all this. I suppose I was on the cusp of something myself. I sometimes wonder if, like me, she ever got 'lines' at our school for reading at the table in the dining hall.

Reader

From those first squiggles I always knew I'd be writer even though I had no idea how I'd get there. The squiggles became words and the words became stories, written in small books made from folded pieces of paper and squirreled away. I began to read. I joined the library and read more. The shapes in my mind joined the shapes of the great novelists and storytellers of literature. At one point at the age of eleven or twelve I was reading six books a week. The girl behind the library desk, Marian Smith, got to know my taste and saved books for me.

So you can see that in serving my apprenticeship to be a writer I first had to become a book-worm. Well, not so much a book-worm as a book-dragon. Once I discovered that it was possible to escape into a book I was hooked. What was I escaping from? Well - start with the drab house, the stressed mother, the bullying at school, the arms and face too long, the hands too big, the hand-me-down clothes, the sparse meals…

From such a dark place I could escape to a ranch in Canada, go on a long trek in China, feed horses on a Scottish farm, sun myself on a Spanish hacienda, dance in a Danish castle, visit a spooky house called Manderlay, sail a boat on Lake Windermere, or enjoy jolly japes at a boarding school in Surrey. Adventure, colour, drama, comedy and tragedy were at my finger tips at the turn of a page. It was fan-tastic. On reflection, my life then could actually define the term *escapism*.

Nowadays there is a school of thought that disadvantaged children should be offered literature that validates and reflects their own environment. I have enjoyed good examples of such literature. We are offered novels like those of David Almond or Alan Garner who do this, in sufficiently complex and multi-layered fashion to be of literary interest right across - and up and down - the snakesandladder board of class and culture. You will have your own favourites that fit this bill.

In those days, though, I did not look to literature for what I already knew. I looked for what I could wonder about: sumptuous rooms, tea on the table and a smiling mother, picnics in the dorm, trekking in the wastes of Canada, murderous wives and predatory widowers, love beneath the oleander tree, walking with a hundred Chinese children to safety, showing courage in the revolutionary wars in Russia, delivering lambs on a Scottish hillside, assassinating kings and sailing with my comrades down Coniston Lake.

So far, so very escapist. But in so escaping I discovered for myself the universals of emotional, political and social life, far beyond the confines of that small house in that small town. I now feel certain that this level of escapism ensured that, for me, as for the Bronte sisters, that though one's domestic life might be contained, the spirit can roam free and the soul is never parochial.

However, being a book-dragon was not without drawbacks. One day at school, escaping the dining hall clatter of plates and voices onto Crusoe's desert island, I was pulled up by my red-haired German teacher.

'What are you doing there, Wendy?'

'Reading, Miss.'

'Two hundred lines! I must not read at the dinner table.'

I must not read at the dinner table
I must not read at the dinner table
I must not read at the dinner table

I do now of course …

A major and surviving element in this *escaping into books* has been my long term appreciation of libraries and people who work in them, like Marion Smith whom I mentioned above, from my early years.

When my first adult novel *Riches of the Earth* was published chartered librarian Gillian Wales invited me to launch it in one of her branch libraries. I thought that very kind, as I didn't know her very well at the time. I was very excited about the book, about seeing my first long adult book in print, so the idea of a public launch was very gratifying.

I didn't quite know what would happen, but Gillian (as I realise now, *typically*) had it all organised. On that day I was 'in residence' in the library in the afternoon, signing books and talking to borrowers as they came through the doors. In the evening I gave a talk and there was wine and welcome to all-comers, including the chairperson of the council, who wore her official chain.

In the library Gillian had organised an exhibition of artefacts that reflected the themes of the novel and, most wonderfully, a cake iced with an image of the cover of the book! I was flattered and delighted by the way in which the library – and particularly Gillian – welcomed my precious novel.

Since then Gillian has become an inspirational friend and has been the creative midwife of all my book launches. Not only that, she has become an important advisor and a true support, discovering sources and coming up with ideas which have often ended up as novels. She was a direct influence for the novel about Mary Ann Cotton *A Woman Scorned* and the novel *No Rest for The Wicked*, about a travelling theatre troup. And she travelled with me to Colorado Springs to visit our mutual friend Judy, which visit inspired an important section of my novel *Honesty's Daughter,* a novel Gillian often says is her favourite. We travelled to Cracow together when I was researching *The Woman Who Drew Buildings*. Her interest and expertise in mining art and the Settlement Movement - she has herself collaborated in the writing of several books on the subjects - inspired me to write *Where Hope Lives,* about a miner who becomes an artist in the 1930s. This is a novel I particularly love.

As well as encouraging me to set up a long-surviving writing group with a series of workshops, she also commissioned me through the years to run a whole range of writing workshops, one of which was *The Determined Butterfly*[1] which focused on writing a novel in a year.

Gillian is a change maker and a great manager. One day I was walking to the Town Hall where she managed the Library, Art Gallery and Theatre. I was feeling very down because my dear brother Tom – an aspiring writer himself and a member of the writing group - had tragically and unexpectedly died of a heart attack. By the time I got to the Town Hall an idea popped into my head about a writing competition in his name. Gillian and I talked and set the idea rolling that day. In the end we ran that competition annually for more than ten years and it had entries from all over England and even some from abroad. As we managed and ran it each year, as well as encouraging writers, which it did, it always reminded me of my dear Tom.

She is still full of fresh ideas and is the best read person I know: among other things, she now reviews books on and contributes to *The Writing Game*, my community radio show. Another enterprise we are involved in – with our friend Avril Joy – is *Room To Write*, a small collective which puts on bi-annual writing conferences for serious aspiring writers and encourages them to aim for publication.

I have been lucky, as a writer, to have such a friend.

Scholar

I reckon now that I must have been a puzzling child to teach. I won my place at the grammar school which – fair or not – in those days labelled me as clever and part of the regional elite. Later, when I was training teachers, I discovered that in my decade, passing for the Grammar School meant that you were in the top 15 percentile of the whole population, with an IQ of between 130 to at least 150.

At school I read in private and in public. I had a peculiarly esoteric fund of knowledge, was curious about everything, could write and listened hard and asked good questions. My drawback was, that I was shy, I looked scruffy, was from a poor background, and was a bit fey.

My English teacher, who never actually remarked on what a good writer I was (I was!), once put *Good syntax* in the margin of one of my essays. I had to look it up to see what he meant, what I was good at. However he never offered to elaborate on it.

My history teacher had me read my essay on Napoleon out *in full* to the class. The reading took the whole lesson. (At the time I was very proud of that. But since then, I've thought that perhaps she'd overdone it the night before and was a bit hung over...)

My French teacher took me to one side and asked in astonishment - nay, disbelief! – how I'd managed the get the equivalent of an A* for my mock French O level. He had been teaching me for five years by then. I did as well in French, German and History A Levels, as well as pocketing my nine O levels. This was not remarked upon, Perhaps they were all in shock.

The only verbal feedback I received was from the same English teacher, even though I hadn't done A Level English. It was the custom then, on the last day before you left school, to go around the teachers who had taught you and say goodbye. I only went in to see the English teacher because my friend Margaret - characterised as *Sandy Cornell* in the story below - had done an English A level with this teacher.

He turned to me. 'Wendy! *You* should have been going to university, you know, to do an English degree!' That was the first proper feedback I'd had in seven years in that school: the possibility acknowledged that I might be clever, might be a writer. Even very clever. Even a good writer. I blushed and smiled and stared at his shiny brown head which was imprinted with a lipstick kiss where his loving wife must have kissed him as he left for school that morning.

I would have liked very much to go to university and do a French degree – not an English degree - but that was a possibility too far. Even so, through my mother Barbara's sacrifices and generosity of spirit, I managed to stay on in the sixth form at my grammar school, and, encouraged by her, went on to two years teacher education in a castle. (Now there's another story.) My mother was stopped more than once in my street and told she was crazy to let me stay at school and go to college instead of getting me out to work to bring money into the house. She often told that story with relish.

So, despite having this rough experience of school I became a teacher of Art and History in a very basic secondary school. As well as teaching Art and History I was in charge of the B Stream in this two stream year. As a very young, very green, twenty year old, I was nearer in age to my pupils than I was to my teaching colleagues. But, even though I grew to love my teaching, by then I was a writer who dropped into teaching, rather than a teacher who happened to be a writer. But you can be sure that, as a teacher I applied the lessons I'd learned in my education by being a very different teacher from the people had who taught me.

As well as my own ability to fantasise and endure, I had survived the stresses of my schooling through an extraordinary friendship with a girl called Margaret. Thirty years later I wrote about Margaret in what I think is a very important short story. In the story I called Margaret by a different name: *Sandy Cornell*. Here is an extract which, when I think about it, demonstrates the closeness of fact, fiction and truth.

From *Sandy Cornell* (In **Knives** Collection 2009): (I could have paraphrased this story to make it pure autobiography but the fictional story tells a neater and more absolute truth…):

…I met Sandy Cornell at the worst time of my life and in retrospect, she saved my life. That I survived to live now, that I have children and grandchildren, that I have endured and enjoyed the adventures of my life, is down to her.

Sandy and I went to this very modern school with plate glass windows: a state-of-the-art-school a brave-new-world-school, an envy-of-the-district school. It was a very working class school, but still a wish-we-were-Eton school. It was a wearing-uniform school, a teachers-wearing-gowns school, a doing-your-homework school, a thank-god-we-won-the-war school.

There was no refuting the fact that I was clever when I arrived there. Placed straight into the A stream, I was seventh in the class which meant seventh in the whole district, where this school was seen as the best school. Despite my dirty hands and scruffy clothes I was still a natural: words and ideas entered through my eyes and ears and found valid connections in the universe of in my brain.

Success in English and French were underpinned by voracious reading of unsuitable material like comics and salacious novels, as well as all the decent stuff. Achievements in History and Geography were underpinned by intense discussions at home where, for hours at a time, my mother and I would forget that the fire had gone out or there was little for supper, and talk. At first, with such excellent home tutoring I could spin ideas, spew words out on the page in some order and get good marks at school.

Scruffy and unkempt though I was, I was taken up by

Alma Simpson, an outstandingly pretty girl who was flirtatious and popular. She mesmerised me. I felt warm in her presence. Later, when our paths diverged, I came to notice that she always took up with outsiders: people who could worship gratefully at her shrine, people who, in contrast with her, were scruffy or ugly or in some other way misbegotten. She shone in such company.

As time went on the most profound feeling I experienced in this school was fear. I was afraid of the teachers: alien creatures whose faces were hard and unreadable, who would punch you and flick you with impunity, and call you by your surname or merely with the epithet *girl*! I was afraid of the boys who were bouncy and brave, whose word for sanitary towels was *jam-rags* and who called you names. (They nicknamed me *Medusa*, after the mythic Gorgon: something to do with my bushy hair.) They cornered you with their energy, so that you wished profoundly to be invisible and began to walk around as though you were. Most of all I was afraid of the wall of work that, though not difficult to me, piled up and remained undone because I went home from school to brood and sleep in my misery, dreaming of invisibility.

My friend Alma, who smirked and looked at her nails when the boys bawled and ragged me, had a miraculous answer for the undone work. No need to worry, she said. 'You know, when the teacher asks you to call out your mark? They don't check. Just say any mark. Not too high. Somewhere in the middle. I'm always doing it.'

So I tried her miracle method and, unlike her, was exposed in my fraud. There ensued the most miserable time ever in my life. I was made to feel as guilty as if I had murdered someone. The headmaster, stout and smelling of sweat, stood there on the stage in front of the whole school, swinging his spectacles on his forefinger. 'I can't fight liars,' he said. 'You know who you are. I know who you are. I can't fight liars.'

I stood there frozen, cloaked in my invisibility and watched him swing those spectacles, his plump little finger daintily in the air.

After that incident I stayed away from school for nearly a term. I wrote my own sickness letters. Nobody seemed to notice. The school didn't notice. My mother didn't notice. I was in my uniform when she went to work, I was in uniform when she returned home and flopped on the couch in exhaustion. For me, this proved I must have attained invisibility. I think that if self harm had been even conceivable then as it is now, I would have cut myself. If I'd had the means or that kind of imagination, I would have ended it all, made myself permanently invisible.

As it was, I knew I had to return to school, to become visible again. More than once I got as far as the big school doors and retreated. One day, when I tried returning to school, I remember looking at the reflection of the dark winter sky in the plate glass windows and feeling that the inside of this place, with its chairs and books and nipping teachers, was an illusion, a dream. For a full minute I was in suspension. I could not go in and I could not go back. The thought chiselled itself into my brain that I had to make choices. I could go inside, or I could go back home and go to sleep. Or, I could walk right down the lane to the river and walk in up to my neck, arms out like Jesus.

No. I would go in, into the school. One foot after another, I forced myself forward. Then I rushed and pushed the door hard. It swung back against a stout body.

The headmaster's currant-black eyes glittered. His salmon-steak cheeks flushed. 'What? What? You, girl! What're you doing?' Spit clung to the corner of his mouth.

I tucked in my chin. 'Coming into school, sir.'

'You've been out?' He smelled of old cheese and toilets.

'Yes sir.'

'It's not *allowed*.' Sweat was running down his temple into his ear.

'I know sir.'

'Why have you been out?'

'I've been home, sir.'

'It's not *allowed*.'

'I know sir.'

'So, why did you go home?'

'I went to put the light under the boiler sir. For the washing.'

'Why? That's your mother's job, to light the boiler.'

'My mother's at work, sir.'

'At work?'

'At the factory. Doesn't get home till five. Then she does the washing, it being Monday.'

A long, unbearable silence. Then he sniffed. 'Don't do it again, girl. It's not *allowed*.'

'No sir.' I looked for a clear way round him but he stood in such a way that I had to squeeze past him. Then I walked right through the school to the back entrance, ran home and lay on the couch, thinking what a mistake it had been to try, to *try* to get back through the glass door.

I *did* go back but that was after the long summer holiday, at the beginning of the new school year. The summer had been a rest from the worry and in September

I managed to force myself back to school properly. In this new world Alma Simpson had taken on a new friend, a whey-faced gangly girl with a receding chin and bottle-bottomed glasses. Beside this girl Alma looked even more enchantingly pretty. I realized then that, as Alma's scruffy sidekick, she had used me in the same way.

That term, in an accident of placing, I sat beside Sandy Cornell, who had skin like a peach and was six foot tall: a dreamy, willowy flower. She was always neat in her uniform and had new pens, pencils and protractors at the beginning of each term. I finally emerged from my fog to notice that, rather than the quiet person I'd thought she was, Sandy was kind, funny and laid back. She made me laugh. We walked with linked arms. I was welcomed into her cosy house by her domesticated, comfortable mother and her hardworking father. At weekends I would retrieve the deposit on returnable bottles just to get the bus fare to visit that family with its predictable routines, its ordinary down-to-earth humour.

Sandy Cornell was the first - although not the last - person I ever met, who used irony as an everyday tool. Untroubled by the fact that she was not overwhelmingly clever, she was comfortable in her skin and was never a target for the exquisite boy-cruelty that had haunted me for years. She smiled ironically at those monsters behind their backs, looked dreamily down at them from her great height. She was obviously no pleasure as a target.

By some miracle, when I was at Sandy's side, the taunts stopped. The fear that had haunted me in my time there receded and my cleverness wound itself into a rope-ladder that helped me climb out of the pit I'd dug for myself. Now I was able to go on and live a visible life....

On the bright side of all this, our scholar *did* go on into teacher training, *did* go on to gain an Advanced Diploma in Education, *did* gain a good Master's Degree in Education (interestingly her dissertation subject was *Language and Power*...) She was asked to go on and do a PhD, but turned down that offer to opt - at last! – to write her first big adult novel and go on to become a full time writer.

Castle

Three things in my life have fundamentally changed and developed my world-view. One was having my son and my daughter. One was working for an extensive period in a prison. The third was the teacher training course I took when I left school. My mother was visionary in encouraging me to do this – at great personal sacrifice. I didn't learn much about teaching there; what I learned was much more important.

Picture this:

Our girl is older now: skinny and intense. She's made it to college and sports a pony tail that holds back her bushy hair. She's sitting by a narrow, lead-glazed, fourth floor window, looking down over a medieval courtyard enclosed by a curtain wall, which in turn encloses trim triangular lawns. Behind her is a very large square room with four single beds, four wardrobes and four chests of drawers. Her quarter of this space would absorb the whole top floor of the little house she left behind just this morning.

In the centre of the room is a long writing table with four chairs; to one side is an elegant, Adam fireplace with a cast iron hearth and a black iron coal scuttle full of coal. The fire is unlit but ready: expertly laid with paper and sticks.

Our girl is reading a woman's magazine in the dying light from the window, evading the fact that she's alone among strangers. The last time she slept among strangers was after her father died, when she stayed with her Auntie Lily, who was something of a psychic. At eighteen she's never even been on holiday but here she is, stuck with these people for five whole weeks. *(No home leave till Half Term* the paperwork says.)

The door opens and in bursts a girl in green wearing her long, black hair in a pony tail. The air fills with the scent of roses. Our girl blinks. This girl has a gleam about her, as though she's standing under a spotlight. 'What are you doing here?' she says, smiling. 'All on your own?' The accent is as soft as rain from the West. Our girl thinks of Lancaster, where her family lived before they moved to Coventry, where her Daddy died. 'I'm reading,' she croaks, waving her magazine. Even through the croak, her tone is sulky, excluding.

The girl in green leans on the writing table in the middle of the room. 'D'you know they call this corridor 'Nursery Corridor'?'

Our girl nods. It was in the paperwork. *Room 11. Nursery Corridor.*

'It's the Kingdom of Children up here!' the girl grins. 'Have you seen the bathroom?'

Our girl shakes her head, thinking of her little house where there's no bathroom; just a zinc bath on a hook in the yard.

'It's big enough for four ducal children, I'm telling you. And water! Gallons and gallons of water!'

Our girl swallows, unable to say anything. Her throat is sealing itself up. A chasm of silence opens up between the two of them.

The girl in green glances around the room then turns her dazzling smile on the girl in the window. 'Look, love, we're having cups of tea along there, a few of us. I've brought me own teapot.' She unties, then reties, her pony tail, pulling on the ribbon. 'I came for you. You should come!' It wasn't a request. 'We're at the very end of the corridor. Up a few steps.'

Our girls nods, then shakes her head, waving the magazine. The girl in green vanishes. Our girl waits a full five minutes, her head in the magazine, before she makes her way along Nursery Corridor, following the laughter.

So she makes friends with the charismatic girl in green. In time her voice returns and her new friend puts soap and sugar poultices on her boils, brought on by eating rich food three times a day – more than she would eat in three days back home.

In time, now part of the group gathering around the girl in green, *our* girl starts to talk and smile. She learns how to link arms and tolerate the touch of others. Occasionally this gaggle of girls finds life so comical that they collapse in a heap, helpless with laughter. The girl in green calls this their *heap of worms.*

Despite the coal fires in the Adam fireplaces, Nursery Corridor is cold and the girls pile on thick jumpers, wear coloured tights and flaunt their red, yellow and blue college scarves like flags. In the vacation our girl takes her new friends to visit her sister – now a happily married woman. Her sister looks askance at the girls, with their coloured tights and their hippy demeanour. She jokes that she'll have to walk ten paces behind them in her city, so people don't think they're with her.

In this cold castle our girl relishes the warmth of the human touch for the first time since her Daddy died, after which she could no longer feel her small hand in his large one, his little finger finding space in the sleeve of her cardigan.

Even here in the warmth and fellowship of the Castle our girl still endures her dark times. This is when she retreats to the chair in the narrow window and writes wild stuff in her notebook, which she shows to no-one. Or – her new joy – at night she'll go alone down four flights of stairs and across the courtyards to paint in The Art Room. This is a wonderful, high-ceilinged space that was once the Castle laundry. Here, as she paints, she sometime thinks she can hear the laundry maids larking around as they wash the ducal sheets.

One girl, on the edge of the group, is here because she's been 'sent down' from the nearby university for having too much of a good time. She tells our girl and her friends that, at the university, most of the girls were *not* virgins. This seemed incredible to our girl and her innocent friends, who are all – well - virgins. They think this newcomer is making it up.

In years to come she'll begin to see this time as – for good or ill - the very end of an age of innocence, not just for her but for her whole generation. But even so, in these two short years, her own heart becomes lighter and her own darkness recedes. In the years to come as well, she'll realise that her time here – the walking across green river meadows and the trekking the long beaches; the writing at the long table; the way they scared themselves with the conjuring up of a girl-spirit from an *ouija* board; the reading of poetry and plays out loud after midnight in the end room of Nursery Corridor; the dark trek across the triangular lawns to the Art Room to paint in the middle of the night – all these things mark for her the true beginning of who she is, and who she will be.

Teacher

From *Land of Your Possession (1994):*

...They sat in rustling silence as Min pinned a large sheet of wallpaper on the blackboard she'd set up at the open end of the horseshoe. She turned to face them. The rustling stilled and every face looked expectantly towards her. She smiled radiantly from one face to another, willing them to be at one with her, to be on her side. She'd used this successful ploy from her first day of teaching, having picked up the strategy from one of her college tutors. The students used to call this woman *The Hypnotist*, laughing at her even while they fell for her. Min had joined in the laughter but she noted the technique which never failed.

It had never failed her either, with any group of people she taught: from the children she normally taught through to the adults whom she occasionally taught, putting to use her own personal interest in drawing and painting.

Now, one by one, she attempted to draw this group under her spell...

Although I taught in schools and colleges for twenty three years I was always a writer who happened to teach, rather than the other way round. I have already said that my teacher education college- though an amazing experience - taught me little about teaching. But I have to say that my pupils at that first very basic secondary school taught me a great deal. To my surprise - after coming out in boils and losing my voice yet *again* - I really enjoyed being in that school with them. I particularly relished the idiosyncrasy and originality of the children of 1B, whose view on the world combined ancient wisdom, innocence and street cunning in equal measure. At eleven years old some of them could neither read nor write so I had to teach myself how to teach reading and writing, to make progress with them. One boy – whom I now realise must have had some form of dyslexia – could read out his own absolutely indecipherable scribble with the flowing style of Dylan Thomas.

Sam, my first short story to get into print (in the magazine *Annabel*), was inspired by a boy from this class who stood on a rusty nail in the school yard. He refused to take off his wellington boot. When I finally persuaded him to remove it, I understood why. He had no socks on and his feet were ingrained with weeks – months - of dirt. So I – this very green girl of twenty myself – had to decide what to do about this. The short story *Sam* – written several years later - sprung out of this event.

I also called on these early experiences much later in my novel *Cruelty Games* which tells the tale of how just such a green teacher handles the experience of having a pupil who kills two younger children, is convicted of murder, and comes back to see her when they are both much older and he is out of prison.

This story came from a range of fragments of my experience: a boy I later taught in my first primary school, the son of a beauty queen, who had an eerie atmosphere of threat about him; a woman I met when I was teaching in higher education who had been the head teacher of Mary Bell and talked of the devastating effect this murder case had on her idealistic staff; a very senior psychologist who told me how often he'd dealt with ambiguous cases where the 'play' of children had led to death. It was years later when these fragments welded themselves together into the fictional story called *Cruelty Games*.

Ian, the central character is abused by his grandmother and likes to play with younger children. Although *Cruelty Games* was published some years before the event, it strangely anticipates the notorious Jamie Bulger case.

From *Cruelty Games* (1996):

'Shall we do Dibs for 'man'?' said Ian.

'Do Dibs!' said Michael.

They made the play with fists. Michael was 'man'.

The game was fast and full of tumbles: noisy shrieks pierced the still air. The increased number of islands improved the game. There was more scrambling, more catching. Two of Ian's islands crumbled under the energy of the catching. The three of them worked together to re-build them,

Ian was content. 'This is my place,' he thought. 'My place.'

After half an hour they collapsed in a heap and went to sit against an outside wall, gasping for breath.

'More chocolate!' said Michael.

Ian pushed the battered packet firmly back into his pocket. 'Nah, I'm saving it.'

'What for?'

'For Sunday afternoon,' he said. He knew his Nana would be out then, on what she called her *errands*. 'Three o'clock. You can tell the time. Can't you?'

'Yeah,' said Michael.

'Bet you can't!'

'I can,' said Jonno.

Ian had his doubts. But then he smiled. 'Right! Listen! The big hand is on the twelve and the small hand is on the three. Three o'clock. Come out then.'

Jonno was relieved. He wasn't always absolutely sure of the clock. Some days it seemed as though he could do it. Sometimes it made no sense at all.

'Both of you, mind! Make sure Mikey comes. Only

works with three of us.'

'Right!' said Jonno.

'Right!' said Michael. 'It was great today, great!'

'Now we've gotta go,' said Ian decisively. 'Your Mam'll have your teas ready.'

The three of them wriggled under the planks, one after the other. The best of friends, they moved out into the night ...

Asylum

Picture this: our girl is silhouetted by a narrow pool of light, balancing on the top of a very tall ladder in a shadowy room the height and dimensions of the great hall of a mansion house. But this is no mansion house; it's the day room in an asylum – by then called a Psychiatric Hospital - in the 1960s. *Care In The Community* had not yet arrived to rescue the long term residents of these places and throw them on the mercy of their families, the streets, the prisons and their intermittently efficient community psychiatric nurses.

The girl is about nineteen. Her Shirley Temple curls are pulled back into the fashionable pony tail and she is not as pretty as she was at three years old. But she's arty – just now learning to teach Art as well as History at her college, which is in a castle. So - being arty – she's been volunteered by her mother Barbara to put up the Christmas decorations in the vast day room at The Hospital where she works. The girl has to work after lights-out as the patients can't be around as she does it. That would be too interesting.

With all her children now grown up, our girl's mother Barbara has escaped from the factory and the dog track, and returned to The Hospital where she trained in the 1930s. The professional energy and urgency of the work here has reignited her spirit and keeps the depression at bay. She loves her 'folks', some of whom were there when she was training thirty years ago. There are many stories to tell here: the many idiosyncrasies - not only of the patients but the staff as well; the interesting conversations with the doctors who respect her. Then there was the snowy winter, when the buses didn't run and Barbara walked most of the eleven miles to The Hospital because the 'folks' would need her and the overnight staff would need relieving.

Tonight, in her pool of light, tacking her home-made, oversize streamers to the picture rails, our girl reflects on the castle where she is a student, and supposed to be learning how to teach. She's learning many things – how to sleep among strangers, how be carefree, how to touch another person with unforced affection, how to talk into the night about books and ideas, how to walk across meadows, along beaches, just for the sensual joy of it. And how to write for pleasure. But, in fact she's not learning much about teaching. It's the children who will teach her how to teach, once she retrieves her voice and gets rid of the boils.

The girl jumps, suddenly becoming aware of a figure in the shadows below the ladder: a sturdy old woman, very upright, with her hands clasped below her substantial bosom. She reminds the girl of her college principal, a deeply clever woman of intimidating demeanour. Perhaps it's the matron. She takes two steps down the ladder and can now see that the woman is wearing a dressing-gown and a scarf tied like a turban round her head.

A patient, then.

'You're doing very well, my dear. Keep up the good work.' The woman's voice is cultured, well modulated.

'Thank you.' She watches as the woman turns and makes her way back down the corridor to the toilets, her footsteps echoing on the linoleum. Our girl knows about this woman. Her mother Barbara has told her about how she was a patient here in the Thirties: a young woman then, sectioned for post partum psychological disturbance after she'd had a baby out of wedlock. Now, *this* is her kingdom. These days she's inhabited by the spirit, voice and demeanour of Queen Victoria and takes special care of a much younger disabled patient whom she sees as a princess, putting ribbons in her hair every day.

That's her story anyway.

Our girl climbs down the tall ladder and drags it five feet further along, the streamers coiling around her neck like a ruff, before trailing to the floor. The ladders squeak as she climbs them again to continue her work. She hopes desperately that her mother likes the way she's done the day room. Although she's only home now in the vacations she has not lost the desire to please her mother and make her happy. The anxiety that crept into her soul when her father died still lurks there, taking her voice and giving her boils when things get too stressful.

Five years later our girl visits The Hospital when there is a Garden Fête – which her mother Barbara calls a *Garden Feet*. Married now, she's brought her own eighteen month old baby to show her the place where her beloved Grandma works. There are crowds here today, enjoying the balloons and the cakes stalls, the Bingo and bowling. Barbara is on duty in a far building and walks briskly towards them, trim in her uniform. She lifts the baby from her daughter's arms and says she'll take her to show her to the 'folks'. These folks are her patients in the geriatric ward who are too fragile, senile, or disturbed, to join in the merrymaking alongside the other patients.

Our girl watches her mother and daughter vanish around a corner of the monumental building. Feeling lost, she whiles away the time wandering amongst the crowds, making up stories in her head about the things she sees around her.

After an age, Barbara and the chuckling baby return. 'They loved her,' she announces. 'They were so very excited. For some of them it was the first time they'd seen as young a creature for thirty years.' She plants a big kiss on the baby's cheek. 'Except for the kittens and birds,' she added thoughtfully. 'They make a lot of fuss of *them*.'

And she bustled off.

Hugging her child, our girl looks after her mother and wonders at the open affection between her mother and her daughter. She reflects on the fact that she cannot ever remember her mother touching or kissing her. It was her father, before he died, who was the one for hugs and kisses. It was her father who would walk with her, hand in hand, his little finger up her sleeve because his hand was too big to enfold hers.

Dancing in the Dark

Picture this: Apart from the ladder in her tights which shows below the short hem of her skirt our girl is feeling pretty good tonight. Her best friends from college are visiting – staying at her married sister's house in Durham – and all three of them are celebrating surviving half a term as proper teachers by going dancing in a local hotel. The ten-piece band is playing swing with just a touch of Rock and Roll. Out girl loves to dance but her devouring shyness means she has no confidence that anyone will want to dance with her. Her friends, after all, are prettier and more at ease than she is and don't get boils under stress.

At school, at last her boils are gone, she has recovered her voice and she has discovered how much she likes the sparkling, anarchic company of the children, if not the more restrained company of the teachers.

Now in the dance hall the lights are down, the silver ball is spinning and out of the shadows emerges a tall dark-haired boy – no, a young man - in a dark suit. The band is playing a waltz. Our girl will discover in time that's all this young man dances; the waltz. He will always say, 'Is it a waltz?'

Amazed that he hasn't chosen her prettier friends she nods numbly when he asks her to dance.

'So how are you?' he says, steering her strongly to the right. His friend is alongside them, steering her pretty friend in the opposite direction. Then they all drink coffee together. One boy says teachers were never like this when they were at school.

She has realised now that she recognises him, this boy and feels amazed that he has recognised her. They'd gone out together once just one time, on her second college vacation when she worked in The Factory. There, he was, 'a young man in a suit', obviously going places: upwards, mostly. In fact, she had thought that when he didn't ask her out again, he was quite beyond the reach of this little student, working for the summer in *Goods Inwards* department.

The Factory – one of the biggest in the region – looms large in her family, just as The Hospital loomed large in the earlier generation. Her mother had worked at The Factory before returning the The Hospital. Her sister works there. Her brother, Tom, works there in *Time and Motion*. (She always liked that image, *Time and Motion*.)

One day, far into the future, she will write a novel about that factory, celebrating this young man's lifelong love for the place. She will always love the way he talks about it, relishing its dramas, its unique workers, its special spirit. The novel, written thirty years in the future, will refer back to these days, where fear, innocence and timidity did not prevent our girl engaging for the first time in a real relationship.

After the dance her friends go back to her sister's house and the sister asks *Where is she? Where is her little sister? Who is she with?* When she hears whom her sister is with, she says. 'Oh, *him*? I know him. She'll be all right with *him*.'

He drives our girl back to her sister's house in his grey Austin car and she still wonders why he's asked her, not her pretty friends. And she wonders how she can so like a boy who doesn't really want to dance, who is so grown-up, As well as this, he's well liked, so laid back, so comfortable in his own skin. In fact, when the time comes, he doesn't even ask her to marry him. One day he just says casually, 'When we are married…'

He knows she's clever but he doesn't know she's a writer until well after they're married. But it's he who - listening to our girl complain about the standard of women's journalism on *The Northern Echo* – urges her to write to the editor and tell him how much better *she* could do it. She doesn't quite do it like that but she does write to the editor and the upshot of that is that eventually she has her own weekly column on that paper for four and a half years.

This brand of journalism – as well as her subsequent life in the academic world – teaches her the value and creative function of strong deadlines which will in the future help her organise her life as a working novelist.

From ***Sandie Shaw and The Millionth Marvell Cooker*** *(2008)*. Student Cassie is working on the lines at the big Marvell Cooker Factory, getting to grips with her workmates. She's had one date with a young manager:

…I'm certain now in my heart that it was Evelyn Laing who Tamàs was rushing off to yesterday, when he ran away from me. And I don't blame him. Taking a walk with me must have been like coming back to the Infants Class when you're in the Juniors. He must have thought me very quaint and bumbling, compared with this Evelyn Laing.

And now, through the corner of my eye I can see him, strolling down the gangway. I don't need to see Tamàs's face; that easy loose walk is now printed on my consciousness. I keep my eyes down on the wiring job, shutting him out of my vision till he gets past. I know he's looking at me. I know he's willing me to look up at him but I don't raise my head. Then he's passed and I allow myself to look at his receding back and the nape of his neck, just where his hair stops.

On the other side of the line Patsy whistles, then lets out a cackle and shouts above the hum of the conveyor belt. 'That's quite a blow off! Has our lovely lad been wrestling you for your cherry, pet?' She winks at me.

I scowl at her, suddenly hating her for the crude mind, that up till now I've quite relished. Karen, on the other side, saves me, 'Leave off, Patsy,' she snaps. 'You can't let things alone can you?'

The merriment drains from Patsy's face and I feel sorry that somehow I've caused a rift between these two friends. 'It doesn't matter, really,' I say. 'He never tried anything, Patsy. Maybe I wish he had. Maybe that's the problem.'

This makes Patsy laugh again. Even Karen's hard face softens.

By The Sea Wall

Picture this: Our writer, now our young mother, is sitting with her back to the sea wall at Alnmouth on the Northumberland coast, surrounded by the detritus of a seaside picnic. The wind from the east is cutting and she wears two ponchos knitted for her in carpet wool - bought as a bargain - by her mother Barbara. Our girl has never liked the cold, suffering blue hands and feet as a child. Later, when she is more than thirty she'll be diagnosed with asthma, the disease that killed her Daddy. When she tells this to her mother, Barbara will say, 'What do you want me to say? Sorry? Because I married the wrong man?' Barbara has mellowed in recent years and is a wonderful grandmother, soft and loving. But it still recurs, the old red haired temper, the bitterness at abandonment.

Our girl loves this part of the world. It's wild and true. She went to college in a castle near here and it's here that she learned to like herself and trust others, got to see the beauty of the countryside for what it is – a gift for the soul. Now, despite the cold, she still glories in the long beach, the panoramic, ever-changing sky, the moody sea punctuated in the middle distance by the spiritual weight of Holy Island.

Just in front of her is her family – her daughter, bottom in the air, nose to the ground, examines tiny crabs in the warm sea pools left by the tide. In the distance her husband and small son play at daring the tide to catch their toes. She likes to see her husband out of his smart suit.

She reflects on how - although she never claimed to be maternal - her girl and her boy have been her delight, her liberation. Through them she has experienced a big learning curve, an ultimate class in what it is to be human. For their safety she's had to abandon her own uncertainties, her own insecurities. She's had to resign from work to have her children and to look after them – no maternity leave in those days. But she loves it. At last she can live without duty or obligation except a duty to love these two, to feed them, to tell them stories. She no longer has to please, to prove she's worthwhile, by being clever despite being poor, by being clever and artistic, despite being not so pretty. By being the *Good Daughter.*

Her children mean freedom: freedom to come and go as she pleases, even if she has to bring a pram with her; freedom to know and learn from these minds so fresh to the world; freedom to be with them when they are awake; to watch them when they are asleep; perhaps most importantly for her, freedom to write when they're asleep. This is the time when she starts to write in earnest - when she writes *Theft,* the book that bounces unexpectedly into publication. At this time, as well, she's writing a thousand words of comment and anecdote every week for the newspaper, which will be read by thousands of people over their breakfast cornflakes.

This is when she finally truly knows she is a writer. This is when she truly knows she's a writer who happens to teach, rather than the other way round.

Money is short, so this interlude can't last very long. Her family needs the money so she will be persuaded back into teaching. First, she goes to a child with spina bifida, as a home teacher (there's another story there…). Then back to the classroom, taking her very tolerant baby son with her for half the day. No matter. She *is* a writer now.

But being with her children has planted deep within her a sensitivity to the fragility of childhood: the way children are fragile at the same time as being tough and enduring, even while their fragility makes them vulnerable to invisible cruelty. Motherhood has made her understand her own child-self more. She can begin now to identify with her mother, so different from herself: now she understands more her mother's passion, her mother's virtue: her mother's anger and sense of loss. Even more, she appreciates the genetic heritage: the psychological energy rolling down through generations of her family – adapting to its times Here, she thinks, is a fundamental framework for her stories.

Sitting in her ponchos with her back to the sea wall, it seems that our girl now knows that she is truly ready to be the writer she can be. She doesn't know it yet but she will go on from here to write twenty three individual, unique novels. They will emerge from these Northern spaces, this Northern life, but will be set in different parts of the country, even different parts of the world. Her list of characters will include children and old people. There will be men and women, fraudsters, conmen, murderers and people of ambiguous virtue. There will be artists and dancers, magicians and psychics – all laced together in separate narratives like the marram grass that holds tight the shifting sand on this long Northumberland beach.

From *The Woman Who Drew Buildings* (2009) Adam goes on a ride to the sea with his new friend Peter who is a musician and a motor bike fiend:

.... Once they were north of the Tyne and into the wild country Peter opened the throttle and let the red monster have its head. They rode on and on, on tarmac roads sometimes following the sea, sometimes powering down empty lanes, sometimes slowing down to make their way through villages and hamlets built of grey stone.

Peter finally pulled the bike to a stop in a village on a promontory north of Bamburgh. The brewing turmoil of the North Sea surged all around them, lapping steel-grey rocks and smashing into the redundant staithes a short distance from a low pub, a building barely distinguishable from the squat stone houses. The air was full of rain that was not quite falling and they were both chilled, so it was a relief to get into the warm public bar with its roaring fire and its smell of last night's beer. Apart from a man leaning on the bar and the young landlady, the pub was empty.

They ordered cheese toasties and took two bottles of beer and packets of crisps to sit on the settle by the fire. Adam's creaking leathers, comforting and secure on the bike, now felt bulky and choking. He unzipped the jacket and eased his shoulders.

'So,' said Peter, slipping his jacket off all together, 'Not on a bike before, Adam?'

Adam shook his head.

'So,' repeated Peter. 'What do you think?'

'Amazing,' Adam searched his mind. 'Like flying.'

Peter laughed. 'I met this bike guy in London, he tells me it's *eating the breeze*. I like that.'

The landlady brought the toasties and smiled at them, one to the other. 'Off the beaten track, then?'

'Just riding around,' said Adam.

'Good day for it.' The landlady nodded at the window where the rain was now lashing down and the line between the sky and the sea had been obliterated.

Adam laughed. 'A bit mad, maybe.'

'Always good to be a bit mad,' said Peter.

...They finished their toasties and beer in silence, watching as the rain softened and the horizon re-emerged.

Peter stood up. 'So we are here by the sea. So we walk by the sea, do we not?' His Polish accent suddenly asserted itself.

They passed a woman perched on a bit of the sea wall in a big Barbour coat and woolly hat, watching a bundled up toddler dig in the wet sand, bottom in the air.

By some miracle the rain had now stopped altogether so they made their way to the edge of the tide, where the sand was hard and their big boots didn't sink in. They followed the tide's edge until the reaching sea barred their way. So they stood still and looked across the surging grey expanse of the North Sea.

Mothers and Daughters

The close, passionate and sometimes difficult relationship between mothers and daughters features in many of my stories through different faces, different characters and different narratives. One prime example of this is *Family Ties*. In this novel we have an old mother with a middle-aged daughter whose own daughter is in her thirties, who in her turn has a seventeen year old daughter. For this novel - a kind of Four Ages of Woman, - I see now that I've plucked distinctive elements from my own life for the second, third and fourth generations of the women in this story. But the oldest woman – perverse, independent, intelligent, secretive, charismatic – most clearly emerges from my deep experience of my mother Barbara. I realise this now, though I have to say I wasn't conscious of this when I wrote *Family Ties*.

From ***Family Ties*** *(2006)* Elderly Kate has had an accident and is staying with her middle-aged daughter Rosa, her thirty-something granddaughter Bronwen, and Bronwen's teenage daughter Lily. Rosa – who writes children's novels - is narrating:

> … When she first came here from hospital Kate was quiet. The hospital had shocked her more than she would admit. That, and the accident itself. The next morning she was up at her usual time and in the kitchen before I could get there. The table was set. The cereals were standing to attention and she was stirring porridge in the pan.
>
> I remembered my father in Coventry stirring porridge in a pan. And how happy I was in the mornings before she came back from her nightshift at The Hospital. I

remembered how, in the bad times at Butler Street, there was no breakfast because she was depressed and anyway she had to be at the factory by seven thirty. And how I fainted in school Assembly.

Anyway, on the first morning of Kate's stay I fled upstairs without any breakfast, mumbling something about getting on with my work. I sat here at my desk and told myself that, at my age, I really shouldn't be running away from my mother.

Since then I've managed to eat the porridge before I flee back upstairs to my study. But here I am, still disturbed by the sound of Kate talking to Bronwen and young Lily, and the click and clatter as she moves my things here and there, mixed with the sputter and sweep of the Hoover. When I go downstairs the place will be tidy and shaved clean and all the ornaments will be slightly out of place. There's no doubt about it – with Kate here, I myself am slightly out of place.

… Of course she started this bad feeling herself, by letting Bronwen have the bag of papers with the Tick Book in it. She knew what she was doing. Tick Book! Ticking bomb! Here I am, sailing along, quite content, then Boom! It all floods back. Those years are on my mind again: hiding in the house like an injured rabbit; dancing behind closed curtains; writing in the Tick Book about how Brock came; battling with all those secrets.

I weep for the child that was me.…

Some Mother's Son

When we heard of a local casualty in the Korean war, or a boy killed in a street accident, or even a murderer sentenced to death, my mother would say. 'Ah well, that's some mother's son.'

As you know now, my father died when I was eight and I never met either of my grandfathers, so the interior life of the male of the species would have been a mystery to me had I not had a son and a grandson of my own. Living alongside them and watching them evolve has taught me a lot about the mysteries of the male psyche.

My children's novel. *The Real Life Of Studs McGuire* was inspired by my son when he was sixteen. This is a crime story, but is really a fictional take on the loyal - even loving - friendship I observed between my son and his best friend. That book must have hit some universals because it sold well here and in both Australia and France. It was on the school curriculum in some schools in the Australian outback. A Swiss schoolchild did a long essay about it. The French title is *Pour Sauver Mon Copain*, which has a certain charm.

My grandson at sixteen was a real source of inspiration in France, when I was writing *An Englishwoman in France,* a time-slip novel which in part follows the adventures of Thibery, an eleven year old boy in Roman Gaul. He was one of the last Christian martyrs and became the patron saint of the mentally ill. I also found elements of my character Thibery in an extraordinary Hellenistic bronze statue called *l'Ephebe,* dating back to the 4th century BC. Dug out of the River Hérault at Agde by marine archaeologists in 1964, this statue has more recently been identified as an early portrait statue of a youthful; Alexander the Great. I have a huge poster of him in my study. This grave young face looks at me across time and I see in it elements of the lives and universal natures of my son and grandson. All manhood is there. In time, this image gave me a strong feeling for the unspoken character of young Thibery in 304 AD in Gaul, as he goes about healing and travels the journey to his martyrdom and eventual sainthood.

From *An Englishwoman in France (2011)*. My narrator Stella has just time-shifted from 2010 AD to 304AD:

….I pull marigolds, daphne, clover - even small sticks of jasmine blossom - from my hair. If my mother could see me now! And there's this bird that must think I'm a bush because it perches on my shoulder and sings *Or ee ole.* *Or ee ole*, its whistling jarring in my ear.

Misou, Madame Patrice's little dog, is still with me. She creeps from my neck down into my sleeve. The bird on my shoulder does not budge an inch.

A dream! It has to be a dream. Or am I really crazy?

Or both. Because here are Louis and the boy, still in their friar's clothing, a kind of long tunic caught up with a rope belt, and a long pointed hood. The sunlight glints off the boy's red-gold hair and he smiles. He smiles at into my eyes.

'Mummy,' I can hear my Siri's voice in my ear. 'Mummy...'

The bird on my shoulder digs its claws into my shoulder and flies away. I feel faint. Louis catches me. 'Madam, how are you?' he says. It *is* Louis. But he sounds different. A dream effect, I suppose.

'Louis!' I say.

'Not here,' he says. 'In this place, in this time. I am Modeste.' He turns to his companion. 'And this is Thibery, known to all as Tib.'

The boy beams at me and it's like a greater light

catching the sun. 'I dreamt of you many times, madam! I saw you and you needed me but we always seemed to pass each other by.'

I look into his eyes. 'Then we were dreaming of each other...Tib. I dreamt of you. I dream of you now.' I like the sound of his name on my tongue but I don't know whether he'll understand me.

Louis reads my thoughts. His voice is in my ear. 'You think he may not understand you. But is it not the Feast of Pentecost?' he whispers. 'All people understand each other. Does not the bird alight on our shoulders with the gift of tongues in its beak?'

What are we doing? Are we dreaming each other? Are we in each other's dreams? I clutch my brow. It's all too hard.

'Don't worry, lady,' says Tib. 'It will be all right. You will be with us. We'll take care of you.'

My character Stella is a woman in the present day who, massively depressed at the savage murder of her daughter, becomes mad enough to see through time.

I'm coming to think now that madness, depression and eccentricity feature as running themes in my stories. Perhaps the obsession goes back to the time I sat on the ladder fixing the Christmas decorations in the asylum. Or perhaps it is something to do with my mother, listening to her talk about her 'folks'. Perhaps it's just growing up in the shadow of The Hospital. No wonder it creeps into the novels.

Also from *An Englishwoman in France (2011)* Here is Stella again:

.... my partner Philip thinks I'm barmy. No, seriously, he thinks I'm mad. The fact is I'm very normal - normal as any of us ever is. And the older I get the more I realise *no one* is normal. Aren't we defined by our abnormality and normal in our own way?

Of course, like most people, I have my own play on what is *normal*. There is this family tradition of seeing the dead. My grandmother's sister, great-aunt Lily, was a medium – you know, one of those people who stand in front of a crowd of people and call up the dead? Me, I see the dead in the more ordinary way of things. I just see people who *shouldn't* be there, in that place, at that time. For me this is the ordinary way of things. It is normal.

These visions can turn up in the most ordinary places; the park, for instance, where I used to walk with my mother and saw a soldier in full World War One battle gear. Then I saw through him to the dusty privet hedge behind him. Then there was that time, in the Spar shop on the corner, when I saw this woman standing behind the woman at the till. She was very old and wore a red sari with gold edges. I could see through her to the serried ranks of cigarettes on the wall behind her. She was like smoke in the air.

And I would regularly see my father standing behind my mother in the bathroom. Not so unusual, you might say. But *he* wasn't there either. She and I subsequently decided the person I saw must have been my father but she wasn't sure. It could be one of four men, she said. 'There were those four wild weeks in 1977 on this campsite in Brittany. They were all nice guys. But, you know,' she added vaguely, 'Ships that pass in the night and all that.'

My mother often relished our shared gift, but she taught me very early on to keep it a secret. 'That kind of thing used to happen to me, love, when I was young,' she said. 'But it kind of faded away.'

Only Connect

From *Riches of The Earth (1991)*:

> Caradoc had climbed onto the train at the very last minute. His view of the carriage was entirely legitimate; it would be the view of the guard, who would come to check the occupants. Four people matched with four tickets.
>
> Now, from her crouched position under the seat, Susanah could hear the train screeching and crunching its way along the track. The wheezing and grinding of the wheels seemed very close to her ear; she thought the floor must be very close to the ground. She pressed her cheek against the wood, wishing she could push clean through. Then she could see the shining iron rails and the stout wooden sleepers as they counted their way north...

'I think we must be related.'

These words sprang out of a letter I received from another part of the country about three months after the publication of my first adult novel *Riches of the Earth*. This novel was completed after I'd finally stopped working as a lecturer - having virtually collapsed from overwork - and had a period where I withdrew from life, could not drive, could not read so much as a paragraph or write so much as a line. I was in a dark place. I had published three children's novels by then – four, if you counted *Theft*, some years earlier. As well as writing these books I had worked full time as a senior lecturer, ran a house and managed my family. My soul couldn't take it. No wonder I found myself in this dark place.

When at last I started to stumble into the light I looked again at the drafted chapters of this novel about Susanah which was inspired by another of those family stories, of how as a child my grandmother Sarah Ellen travelled North from Wales with her family, because her father had got a job as a miner. They travelled by train and Sarah Ellen had to travel under the seat, as they only had tickets for four of the children. The story went that her father was very severe and forbidding: an old style patriarch. Although virtually illiterate, he was a clever man. He worked full time in the pit and hammered tinned goods which he sold in the community. Very frugal and virtuous in his habits, he accumulated money and acted as a money-lender for his more self- indulgent workmates. He went to collect his pay at the pit in a pony and trap, which was seen as very above himself.

Sarah Ellen had to run off to marry because he wanted her to stay to mind the house and the younger children, because his wife, Sarah Ellen's mother, was fragile with a secret weakness, they said, for fruit wine.

When Sarah Ellen's husband, Tom Blair, was killed in the First World War her stern father occasionally threw some charity her way - such as half a dozen pairs of boots, delivered from the Co-op store. My mother Barbara, Sarah Ellen's middle daughter, got into trouble because she wouldn't wear the boots. She said they were for boys, not girls. She went without dinner for a day for such impudence.

These vestigial stories were all I knew about the early life of that family but, before I got ill, I had set about inventing a long novel, stretching from 1895 to 1921. I wrote *Riches of The Earth,* inspired by, but not based on, Sarah Ellen's story (I have called her *Susanah* in this novel). In the novel Susanah's narrative is counterpointed with that of Jonty, a young teacher who led a group of pacifists called the Quebec Radicals in East Durham. But even Jonty has his truth. He is also based on a real person, a gifted young preacher whose documented story I found in the Durham County Record Office. He was a man of intelligence and courage.

Recovering from my illness, I got stuck half way through this novel, wondering whether I had the stamina – or the writing skill – to complete the large task I'd set myself. Looking for encouragement, I went to a writing retreat led by the late John McGahern, the wonderful Irish writer of *The Dark* and *Amongst Women*. When he saw my sample chapters from *Riches of The Earth* he laughed. 'Sure, you are joking!' he said. '*Of course* you can write. You're a *great* writer.' We had some absorbing conversations there at Lumb Bank, comparing notes as writers on the dark inspiration of our backgrounds. He told me a tale of his father beating him with barbed wire, which was too terrible to find its way even into his dark novels.

So, permission given and confidence restored, I went on to complete this novel, which sold to the first publisher to whom it was offered. Of course it was labelled as a *saga* as were the novels which followed it – even though some of them were not technically sagas. This was always a source of regret to me.

Let's get back back to this letter from the stranger, which said '*I think we must be related.*' The writer recognised 'Caradoc,' Sarah Ellen/ Susanah's fictional father in the novel. '*You have him to a T. His voice, the way he went about,*' my correspondent wrote. In fact I had made up all of these things about Caradoc, who entered the novel from the fringes of those family stories that I'd overheard, and took off on his own: a fully rounded fictional character.

In correspondence with this lady I discovered that what she said was correct. Although twenty years younger she, like Barbara, was actually also the granddaughter of the old man – the product of the late marriage of one of the two bachelor sons whom the old man had kept at at home well into middle age. (Sarah Ellen was definitely the one who got away…)

This woman's letters eventually showed me a whole other side to the old man, a softer, gentler side that made me understand more that iconic character from my family's history. It made me realise that people do mellow in older age. My mother certainly did, in her warm love for her grandchildren.

Yet in all the family tales I listened to from my mother, this connection in her grandfather's family was *never* mentioned. This was a small community so she and her sisters must have known about the woman, at first a housekeeper, who was partnered with her uncle and who had a daughter (their cousin) who became my correspondent. Neither the mother nor the daughter were part of Barbara's version of her family's history: a truth lost; a story re-told in fiction.

Alas, by the time I heard about this relationship, Barbara was gone from me and I couldn't check out this story with her. I can't believe it was a secret even from her. But in time I have discovered that alongside the tales, told and retold many times, there were other secrets, kept close for reasons of convention, propriety or hypocrisy. Perhaps these secrets are part of the social contract within families to keep the surface of family life smooth, bearable, without being disturbed by ripples of revelation.

Although I have never really put it together properly before, I now see that this sense of secrecy within families crops up again and again in my novels. Certainly it is very important in *Family Ties*, and it is at the core of a later novel *The Woman Who Drew Buildings*.

One postscript to this story of the letter: I eventually met this lady, my mother's secret cousin, at a book event. We had a warm conversation and were comfortable together. She knew all about Barbara and her sisters, which made me think even more that *they* must have known about her. But the thing that stayed with me was how much she resembled them them all, particularly Barbara and Auntie Louie, the one who knitted the Fair Isle cardigans for us when we were small.

Sometimes I think that Fact beats Fiction into a cocked hat…

Even so here, to continue the theme of *family secrecy,* is an extract from fiction - from ***The Woman Who Drew Buildings.*** Adam is 22. He's come home after two years in prison to find his mother in a coma. He has left her in hospital and returned to her new flat:

> Adam took his empty plate through to the kitchen, rinsed it and left it to dry: old habits die hard. This might be a new place but it was still Marie's kingdom and her rules counted. Then he took a second bottle of wine from the fridge, got a new notebook from the pile in her bottom-left desk drawer, came back and began to make a careful

list of the things that had spilled out of the boxes. His face was burning with wine drunk too fast, his brain was racing, his hand was shaking, but one by one he listed the items from the brown cardboard box.

- Article in Esperantist magazine by Marie Mathéve, recounting her 'Study In Poland.'
  - A newspaper article about the visit of Marie Mathéve's visit to Poland on a Siropotimist grant to consider buildings
  - Photo of Marie and a younger woman leaning towards each other, making a triangle. On the back Marie has written; Jacinta Zielenska and me.
  - Small published book of drawings of Krakov marked Ex Libris D. Adama Zielenski. Paperback with a brown paper cover to protect it
  - Photographic slides and viewer, small and hard to see
  - Poland's Progress, edited by Michael Murray first pub 1944 this the third ed 1945
  - Krakow, by Edward Hartig 1964. Coffee table book.
  - Poland, by Irena and Jerzy Kostrowicki
  - Official 1981 guide to Krakow
  - Official guide to Katowice
  - Notebooks
  - Two small red Sylvine notebooks still with their 30p price tag on. Marked Poland Diary 1981
  - One Winfield exercise book marked Paris Diary 1985
- Daler Sketchbook full of Marie's drawings e.g. : Cherrzov From My Bedroom; steelworks; estate with Tabac in foreground; old steelworks; coal mine looking towards Katowice; done in

coloured markers, making her usual style bright and bold. But style is unmistakable

- *Spiral Bound Daler Sketchbook with more subtle drawings from Brittany, Paris Luxembourg Gardens, View from my window 8th floor Rue de Rennes, Paris. Louvre 1985*

Adam surveyed his neat list. Marie always documented her journeys. Her journals, the articles, the artefacts had always been kept, boxed, listed and cross-referenced in box files on specially built shelves in their old house. When she was away he had sometimes taken them down and leafed through them, admiring her scholarly approach, her crisp writing style. Those boxes must be in storage somewhere. Here in the flat there were no shelves, no lines of box files, no cross referenced filing boxes, just this higgledy-piggledy pile of stuff that had been dumped in boxes and never even entered into the Marie Mathéve system. This material was either too important or too unimportant to her for that. He'd never heard of any journey to Poland. This journey was unknown to him.

'Marie how could you?' he whispered. He looked from the piles to the list in his hand and back again and his eyes burned as though they had been invaded by smoke. Tears spilled down his cheeks. 'What's all this about, Marie? What?'

He was crying again.

Chickens

Picture this: the little girl is about six. Her hair is straighter and thicker and she's quite leggy. They're already calling her *daydreamer*. She's a little bit frightened of her bustling mum but she really loves her Daddy. She likes it when he holds her hand as they go down the road to the shops, his long little finger up her cardigan sleeve. She's proud of him because he makes aeroplane engines at his factory and sometimes he draws pictures for her, of engine parts. He reads the newspaper every day and she climbs onto the cavern of his knee and reads it with him. She likes the comic strip and one Christmas he cuts out a year's cartoons, sticks them on brown paper squares and sews them into a book for her. This is the first book which is her very own.

The little girl knows that her father, like her, is a bit of a dreamer. There's the time when he builds a pen at the bottom of the garden and buys a dozen chickens to rear for eggs. They sit on the back doorstep and he swings a pendant over the fluffy chicks to see which are girls and which are boys. But the pendant turns out to be a liar because the chicks are all boys, so there'll be no eggs. There will only be chickens for eating. But Billy cannot bear to wring their necks, so he has to give them away and the chicken pen in the garden lives on as a monument to a lost dream.

She loves the evenings when her mother has gone to The Hospital for her nightshift and there is just him, and the ticking of clocks, the rustle of papers and the clipped voices on the wireless.

These are the best times, before *he* vanishes.

The Electrician

I sometimes think that whereas we know women through their emotional impact on us, we know the men in our lives best by what they *do*. I know that now because I've lived with a man for two thirds of my life and I have a son and a grandson.

After my father died when I was eight, grown men were conspicuously absent from my life. I knew my gentle, affectionate father all too briefly. But still, his aura has crept into my stories where gentle thoughtful men were needed. He is there as Roland in *Land Of Your Possession,* my novel which starts with the Coventry November Blitz. My parents and their two older children were there during that period. I was nearly born there. In the novel the parents are Lizza (resurrected full of beans later in her life from my first big novel *Lizza*) and her husband Roland.

Roland, like Billy, my father, worked as an electrician on aero engines in Coventry. Shortly after the Blitz the aeroplane factory – and our family – were evacuated to the comparative safety of Lancaster, where I was born. In the novel Roland and Lizza have just one fictional child, Rebecca.

Here they are during an air raid...

From **Land of Your Possession** *(1994):*

.... Of course Lizza had to disturb Rebecca to get her down into the narrow space under the stairs which Roland called a cellar. But the child hardly woke up at all. She just lay across Lizza's lap like a piece of seaweed. The new baby stirring inside Lizza was much more wakeful, absorbing into her growing brain her mother's s restless worry, her battened down instinct to flight.

Roland took the bombing in his usual calm stride. More than once Lizza had thrown a pot at his head in sheer frustration at his lack of panic. In violent rows she'd accused him of insensitivity, of hiding away from the death that was around him.

If he was at work during a raid, he did his shift as a fire-warden there and usually stayed till the all-clear. When he wasn't at work, after doing his fire-warden round, he would return to the house. Then, sitting under the stairs with a torch, or bravely up at the kitchen table, he would make his charts, complete with date, type of aeroplane, frequency and target. The next day he would check his facts as he went to work on his bicycle, crunching across the broken glass, wobbling around the potholes, the crevices and the rubble. When he came home at night he would take an india-rubber, rub out his errors and replace them with verified facts, and ink them in. Then he would add new data about particular streets and buildings that had been hit. His next task was to add sham figures of men and women, like bundles of sticks, in rows, like soldiers. These were his dead.

Lizza didn't need her hospital text books to see that in the wild chaos of death, fire and great explosion, this activity gave Roland a sense of shape, order and control. His neat graphs, his lines of little men, his codes for time and type of plane – all these gave him a quiet man's sway over those giants: those wizards in the sky who, like Thor, could cast thunderbolts into the lives of lesser people...'

Research in the Coventry Archives allowed me as the writer to access the practical truths of life in the Coventry Blitz, but the fact of Roland/Billy making clever graphs and records of the Coventry Blitz is an unadulterated truth. I remember seeing the papers once but they have fluttered out of our lives on our way back north, as did many other precious things. But only now, reflecting here, do I see that by digging deep into my memory-before-memory I've conjured up in this novel something of the truth of the relationship between the fiery, obstinate, clever Barbara and the gentle, conciliatory, inventive Billy. And as well as this I've imagined my own embryonic self stirring inside my mother.

Billy died aged thirty seven and it seemed that all that was gentle, reflective and overtly affectionate bled out of our lives for a long time. We children were told of his death by our father's sister, Auntie Mim, a woman we barely knew. She brought us rare shop-bought cream cakes. I couldn't eat mine but my older brother said eagerly he would polish if off. We went to school as usual that day. Later I was walking home and a neighbour leaned over the gate and asked how my daddy was. 'Oh,' I said airily. 'He's dead now.' Many decades later I can still see her shocked face.

We weren't allowed to go to the funeral. It wasn't the done thing then.

From *Family Ties* (2008):

> … (Auntie) sat us down, dribbled honey over our porridge and then said, 'Little loves, I have to tell you something.' Tears welled up in her eyes. Funny to see a grown-up crying. We sat watching her, our spoons poised.
>
> 'Well, my loves, I'm afraid you won't see your Daddy again.' The tears were flowing down her cheeks now.
>
> 'Not ever?' said Charlie, shovelling a spoonful of porridge into his mouth.
>
> I remember Auntie's black curls trembling as she shook her head. 'No. Not ever. Not in this world anyway.'
>
> Not in this world? I thought of the sky where the Kingdom of Heaven was located, according to Judith Meadows. I put down my spoon and didn't eat my porridge, although the boys ate theirs and Charlie finished off mine.

We were kept off school that day – a long, weary day with lots of coming and going, I spent the day in the garden down by the hen house, wrapped up in my coat and scarf against the sharp February wind. I looked up at the sky and thought how very, very far away the Kingdom of Heaven must be.

... And years later I remembered again my father in Coventry, stirring porridge in a pan. And how happy I was then. Before *she* came back from her nightshift at the Hospital. I remembered how, in the bad times at Butler Street, there was no breakfast because she was depressed and anyway she had to be at the factory by seven thirty. And how I fainted in Assembly.

The Soldier

The heroism of Tom Blair, Barbara's father and Sarah Ellen's husband, reverberated all the way down the twentieth century into our generation. Like my father Billy, Tom Blair died in his late thirties. But he didn't die on a bed in a Coventry Hospital - he died in France in 1918, somewhere near Mont St Quentin, situated on a bend of the River Somme, north of Peronne.

Mont St Quentin was captured by the Australian 2nd Division on the 1st September 1918. Our family eventually discovered that Sarah Ellen's husband, Tom Blair – a Durham Light Infantry soldier - died in that area in mid September. The mantra that echoed down from 1918 into the 1960s was. '*What a waste! He was in it from the day war broke out and died six weeks before the November 11 Armistice. Shame*.' I heard that so many times, couched in the same words.

Tom's body was never found. Sarah Ellen, like many wives in that position, did not believe he was dead. I remember seeing copies of correspondence with the British Legion - politely and determinedly asking for proof - right into the 1920s. The legend was that Tom could have been injured and lost his memory. He was wandering round the silenced battlefields, she was sure. Like others in this family Sarah Ellen was something of a mystic and felt Tom was there, waiting for her to find him. The letters show that Sarah Ellen had a flowing, accurate hand. She was known as a good writer and wrote letters to the Front for her less literate sisters and sisters-in-law. One of these women told me that at my wedding.

Like most soldiers in that war Tom was not really a soldier; he was a miner from a family of Scottish miners who had settled in County Durham. So it seemed that this family was a mirror image of the Evans family, Sarah Ellen's people, who migrated from Wales to work in the pits here in the late 1890s.

The Blairs were carrot-tops with freckles and pale skin. The Evans family had very black hair and pale faces. Barbara inherited thick burnished auburn hair from the Blairs, as did my own sister. The sharp cleverness and creativity of both Welsh and Scottish Celtic heritage has filtered right down to this twenty first century generation: all of our children demonstrate it. We're all clever in our own ways and in our own ways can make and invent things.

My thing, of course, is stories, the making of stories.

It seems to me that Tom Blair had always looked up beyond the pit for new horizons. The reason why he was actually *in* the army the day war was declared was because he was in the Territorial Army, on short leave from the pit. Being in the Territorial Army was a way of spending week-ends and annual leave above ground in the open air. It was also lucrative – and the money would have been welcome in this household which already included five children, the youngest at that point being Barbara, my mother. He must have had some home leave before he finally embarked for France in 1915, because two more Blair children were actually born during the war.

One of Barbara's stories was how, aged three, she was toddling down the long, wide colliery street where they lived and saw a row of men 'on their hunkers' – squatting with their backs against a pub wall. One of these was a soldier and although she didn't recognise him she knew he was her Daddy, just home on leave, his knapsack beside him. He reached out to pull her to him and kissed her auburn curls. Then he gave her a big shiny apple and said, 'Now, flower, you go back to see your Mammy. I'll watch you all the way.' Half way home she looked back and he waved at her. So she turned and ran the rest of the way home.

This is a true story from 1915, distilled and preserved by word of mouth, and existing now in the twenty first century on this page, Barbara's stories often included dialogue.

From **Riches of The Earth** *(1992)* In my story Davey - like Tom Blair - joins the army to escape the pit, but he abandons the pit much earlier, in 1905. Here he explains his reasons to his more political friend Jonty:

... 'Something in particular, Davey?'
'I was talking to this feller down the football yesterday.

On leave from the army, he was. He said he'd take me with him down to Wrexham and join me.'

'Serious, are you? Going in the army and leaving here?'

'Here has nothing for me Jonty. Just the pit. And my father, who doesn't give a light for me. Nor anybody else.'

'What about Susanah?'

Davey ignored the question but said, urgently, 'Go on, tell us what you think of the idea, go on!.'

'You know my views Davey. You know them!'

'Tell us again!'

Jonty sighed. 'Kings and emperors, prime ministers and potentates use the bodies of men like pawns in a game of chess.' He chanted his litany. 'And what king are you to fight for, Davey? A feller that loves pleasure, looking to his own interest. Never away from the races or the gambling tables or the company of women.'

'But there has to be an army, Jonty. Every country has an army to defend itself.'

'In India?'

'It's our Empire. We've got to defend it.'

'The King's Empire is a dangerous place, Davey. Men are treated like so many cattle whether you are one of *us* or one of *them*. You could get killed, get hurt, or die of some dangerous disease, even if you don't get into battle.'

Davey stood up in front of the fire which was roaring nicely now, 'Do you know what it's like down the pit?'

'I think I do.'

Davey snorted like a horse and chanted his own litany. 'Well, schoolteacher, how about when your heart beats the cage to the bottom, as it sinks like a stone? How about the beginning of a shift when it feels like it'll be an age before the shift'll end? How about when it's so bliddy hot that the dust is solid in the air and you feel like you can bite it off in chunks? How about the corners down there where all you can smell is other men's piss and gas that with a bit of luck isn't poisonous? The heat, the dirty sweat, the sheer stink of it! How about working on your knees, hewing coal, hour after hour? How about getting home too tired to eat?'...

The Auctioneer

I have this photograph of Tom Wetherill, the *other* grandfather whom I never met, whose son Billy was my father. In the photograph *this* Tom is about nineteen years old, with a handsome, full face and large smiling eyes. He's wearing a white wing collar and a long evening coat. Very Oscar Wilde. Tom Wetherill had great charm. My mother Barbara called him 'the old man' and loved him. She loved this photograph because it has a touch of class, it hints of better things. It also backs up her story of how he – therefore *we* - came from *better things*. Even in our poorest times she was nothing if not aspirational.

Tom's Wetherill's father was an affluent bailiff, auctioneer and valuer from Ripon in North Yorkshire and the Wetherill family lived on one of the better streets in the centre of this cathedral town. Tom was a very clever boy and the legend on his Ripon Grammar School report was often quoted to me: *Remarkably clever but abominably lazy.*

Reflecting on this now I think perhaps he too was a dreamer like me. *A Romancer*. In my experience we can irritate the more active, task driven people. I think Tom must have worked for his father for a time. But then the story goes that when Tom was seventeen, his parents died and he and his sister were each left three thousand pounds. Depending on how you calculate it, in present day values this varies between £239,000 using the retail price index, to £1,280,000, using average earnings. My mother told me that by the time he was twenty one, little was left of what was, by any reckoning. an enormous sum of money.

How did Tom Wetherill manage that difficult feat you may say? I have no record of this, oral or otherwise. I suppose he could have been swindled or defrauded. But I feel the reason for this great loss was due to a certain weakness that has come down through the generations. There is a gambling streak around this family. It's not impossible that he went off to London or Monte Carlo and tried the tables. From his young photo he looks flamboyant enough. This Tom Wetherill was a gambler, His son Billy was a gambler, My much loved late brother – also Tom - was a gambler. What about me, then? When you think of it, assuming one can *write* for a living is a bit of a gamble. Each novel I write is a 'bit of a gamble'. As well as that I'm prone to taking leaps in the dark. Deciding to work in prison was one of those leaps. As you will read later here, that turned out to be an intensely rewarding experience but it could have been a great mistake.

I don't really know what my grandfather Tom Wetherill did after he lost his money, but I do know that after some years he ended up working in an asylum called Winterton in County Durham. On his wedding certificate he is called *asylum attendant*. (This is the same asylum where many decades later I was up the ladder doing the Christmas decorations…) In time he became chief male attendant. They didn't call them nurses in those days.

At that time the staff – including the doctors – lived on the site, in houses and cottages on the perimeter of what effectively was a large, purpose-built institution. It was at The Hospital (as they called the asylum) that Tom met his wife Elizabeth Ann, who was on the domestic staff. (She once told me that my grandfather had chased her round the table in the Hospital kitchen till *she* caught *him*…)

My father Billy and his sister Alice, called Mim - she of the cream cakes on the day he died - were born and grew up at The Hospital. They were both clever, and both of them went to Stockton Grammar School. Billy lost schooling because he was asthmatic and took an electrician's apprenticeship at The Hospital. This asylum was, for its time, very progressive. It had all kinds of social events – dances, concerts, a drama group, sports teams, chess clubs – in which both patients and staff participated.

Sixty years later I talked to two elderly women who had worked at The Hospital at that time. They remembered Tom and said how much they liked him. He was, they said, a *true gentleman*. He was kind and good at his job. He could play the piano and they enjoyed many sing-songs in my grandparents' hospital house in a square called The Cottages. They recalled with affection New Year's Eves, when the staff living in the cottages would join forces and drink in each others' houses, from glasses they took with them from house to house. Writing this, I'm wondering if, at those parties, my grandmother Elizabeth Ann declaimed what (I discovered much later) was an ancient Durham Mummers Play, normally performed in houses on New Year's Eve? She made us learn it off by heart. I quote it here, as I learned it from her as a child.

In steps King George!

King George is my name

With sword and pistol by side

I hope to win the game

The game sir?

The game sir!

Take your sword and try sir!

Oh dear oh dear what
have I done?

I've killed my father's only son!

Send for the five pound doctor

There is no five pound doctor

Send for the ten pound doctor.

In comes good old Doctor Brown

The best old doctor in the town,

What can you cure?

A dead man to be sure!

I have a little bottle
in my inside pocket

That goes tick tack

Rise up dead Jack!

Oh my brother's come alive again

We'll never fight no more

We'll be the greatest brothers

that every were before

With a pocket full of money

And a barrel full of beer

We'll wish you a merry Christmas
and a Happy New Year

The roads are very clarty,
me boots are very thin,

I've got a little pocket for
to put me pennies in,

If you haven't got a penny
well a ha'penny'll do,

If you haven't got a ha'penny

God bless you.

This grandfather Tom Wetherill died before I was born. Although his wife Elizabeth Ann was on the periphery of our lives for many years afterwards, this ancient play is all I know about this grandmother. Oh – there's something else: she taught us how to play whist, so it would make a 'four', so she could play cards on her visits. And she insisted that the wireless had to be tuned to the racing. And then there was the juvenile mortification when she visited us and – just off the Primrose bus from Lancaster, where she lived - she asked me to put on sixpenny double bets at the bookie's. She favoured a jockey called Scobie Breasley.

On reflection perhaps the reason why I know so little about her - why she is not a person to me - is because my mother Barbara had no time for her, so apart from a few sour allusions, there were no stories.

As I said there was a substantial sporting programme at The Hospital. I do have a rare photo of my father Billy in his twenties. He's in tennis whites, holding a tennis racquet, standing alongside a slim, dark haired woman – not my mother. But Barbara *did* encounter Billy for the first time at The Hospital. She went there to train and work as a nurse in the early Thirties. It was there that they met – an ambitious, fiery young nurse and a smart young electrician, whose gentleman father was on the senior staff. I have a photo of them at that time – he tall, dark and very handsome, she smaller, more rounded with that lovely head of hair. They look happy.

Very occasionally fathers and daughters slip into my fiction. For these I dip into my own experience of a lost father and also my experience of watching my daughter with her own devoted and much loved father.

From *The Lavender House* (2007). Sophia, the narrator, has moved to London to train as a journalist and has met Bobbi, a young girl who lives alone with her father in a Georgian house converted to three flats. Sophia had been dreaming of black tulips in her friend Julia's garden, which were really – she knew - purple:

'Not black,' I muttered again as I opened the door.

It was Bobbi.

'My Dad's not home,' she said, walking straight into my living room. 'I waited and he didn't come.'

I glanced at my watch. 'You should be at school.' My mouth was dry and my head was raging. 'It's eleven o'clock.'

'I never go to school till he's back home from his night work. He did leave me this message telling me not to worry. But when people tell you not to worry you know you should be worrying. Mr and Mrs Selkirk are out and Mr Copeland has gone to work so I came here.' She collapsed onto the couch. 'It was Mehmet's or here. And Mehmet'll be busy with lunches.'

'Ring your dad now! Try again!' My shrill voice hurt my own ears. I rushed to the sink, poured myself a long glass of water and gulped it down.

Bobby stood looking at me. 'You've got a hangover!' she said soberly.

The child knew too much. At that moment I quite disliked her.

'Ring him now!' I repeated. She took out her dinky phone, hit a single number and held it out to me. Straight to voice mail.

'I'm gunna go up West and find him,' she said, pocketing her phone.'

... Which is how Bobbi and I, face now washed, hair brushed, found ourselves in front of a narrow dark green door in an alley behind the Brompton Road that smelled of fish.

The door opened and we were staring at this woman whose over-made up face was too large for her body. She could have been anything from forty to seventy, 'Yes?' she said.

'My dad,' said Bobbi, 'He works here and didn't come home. I've come to get him. You know – Sparrow Marsh.'

'Sparrow?' The woman pursed her lips, deepening the wrinkles around them. 'Sparrow's long gone. You say you're his kid? You're not like him. Not so dark. Went off early. On that bike of his.'

'But I tell you he didn't come home.' ...

The Pitmen

From **Where Hope Lives** *(2001)* Gabriel, the young pitman painter, reflects:

> When I'm feeling low, this blackness is the worst of the pit. Then it seems that this black is the blackest of blackness, the essence of absence. Pitmen have a word for it down there. They call it the *goaf*.
>
> But in the end you get to see wonderful colours down the pit, believe me. Just a flicker, a touch of light from your lamp liberates colour from the *goaf;* that intense blackness behind blackness which is the eternal night of the pit. Underground I learn to feast my eyes on the purple sheen slicked across the seam of coal, the glitter of Fool's Gold; the red of a man's inner mouth; the flutter of the silver-grey moth surviving still down there and the skittering of blind mice rolling like grey feathers along the rails ...

When my Daddy died, Barbara, then aged 36, brought her four children – then aged 13, 11, 9 (me...) and 7 – 'home' to the North. Apart from hospital training and early married life she had not lived in the North since she was fourteen. Her family encouraged her to come 'home' in her hour of need. They found her a two up and two down house with no bathroom, no hot water, no garden. No nothing. A bit of a contrast for all of us. In Coventry we'd lived in a brand new 'jerry-built', mortgaged house with its three bedrooms, its bathroom, its hot water and its long garden with the chicken run at the end. Before that we lived in a similarly comfortable house in Lancaster.

And the myth of the close family who would help her in her hour of need fizzled away before her own savage pride in not seeing herself as a charity case and their assumption that once she was 'home' she would naturally be all right. She wasn't.

So here we have some objective support for Barbara's depressed perception that not only had she the tragedy of a young husband lost far too soon to deal with and - having fought hard to make a better life for herself since she was fourteen - she *had* really come down in the world. She always saw the North as *worse* and the South as *better*. I have since learned she was quite wrong in this but then at the grand age of nine I went right along with her. Her word was my Bible.

My older brother Tom was entranced when he saw the three pit heaps that dominated the town. 'Look at them! Is that where the cowboys ride?' Around the town there were four or five working pits which needed a great number of pitmen to work them.

The word *'pitman'* is most commonly used round here, referring back to the Old English usage rather than the more Norman French miner *(mineur)*. When we arrived our ears were bombarded with dialect words which I now realise were pure Old English intermixed with Scandinavian. The word that some of them used to describe their own language as 'pitmatic'. This language was hard to understand but my brother Tom soon learned it, as he was beaten up at school for *tarken posh*. I, with my head in my books, didn't see the need. My mother – depressed as she was - thought talking like that was the first step on a slippery slope to Hell and fined us a ha'penny for using dialect words or missing the g's from the end of words or the 'h's from the beginning. The lack of ha'pennies made this gesture more symbolic than real.

From **The Making of a Man** in the **Knives** collection. This story was commissioned by the Woodhorn Mining Museum and emerges out of my research into the documents and artefacts in their collection. It's 1913 and young Ralph is reflecting on how he started as a pitman:

> ... My own dreams of a life in the navy flew out of the window when a stone roof fell on my father in this very pit where I work now. Death is in the way of things in the pit.

Only two years ago thirteen men perished here in an explosion. It's just a year since my father was shot-firing a section of stone to clear the way back to the seam. Well, the same stone that he lovingly drilled and fed with gunpowder crashed down on him and his *marrow*, his best mate. Neither of them survived the two hours it took to carry them out-bye, twelve men taking turns at this arduous task.

So, though I was a good scholar and liked school I had to leave and come here to work at this same pit. My mother told me this was necessary: the only way to hang onto the colliery house that shelters her and me and my brothers and sisters: eight of us in all. At first, being so young, they kept me on the surface, picking stone on the screens. But I always knew the only place for man's work is down below. That's where the respect and the better money is. And better money I need because the pittance I got from picking stones on the screens has barely kept my Mam and my brothers and sisters from the workhouse.

There is this special language in the pit. *Pig's tail rope clip, ham bone rope clip*, I am to learn about these things seeing as on-setting is to be my first job underground. Today I will learn about onsetting. And I'll learn about picks, shovels, drills and props, seeing as I am set to be a real pitman and maybe even end up as a hewer, like my Uncle Jonna...

Of course the culture of the pit was deeply embedded in my extended family. My grandfather Tom Blair was a pitman before he was as soldier. His eldest son – another Tom - worked in the pit from the age of 14 to the age of 62, non-stop. He was a highly intelligent man who could talk lyrically about the geological strata under Durham's rolling hills and could read the seams like a text book. The lives of other uncles, cousins and their families in the next generation were built around the pit. They were mostly men of intelligence and prided themselves in their high craft. In more privileged generations they would have been doctors, teachers and lawyers. In their generation the pit, it seemed, was the only option, as it was for Ralph in my story.

My mother Barbara, however, did not respect that tradition. 'No son of mine,' she said more than once, 'will work in that filthy hole in the ground.' Her time away had freed her from the romantic hero-worship of these hardworking men, as well as the domestic slavery that it imposed on the women in the family. She was an emancipated woman who knew her own worth. For many wives of pitmen their men-folk *were* their work. They were high maintenance men. One aunt told me she was the only person she knew whose work doubled when her husband retired. She also warned my seventeen year old daughter never to marry. 'You'll never call your soul your own!' she said, with only the barest twinkle in her eye.

Extract from **Shifts,** a short story set in 1936, also commissioned by the Woodhorn Mining Museum. In it, forty year old Vi, married to the grown up Ralph from the earlier story, talks about the first shift on her twenty four hour working day, built around the three shifts her men folk worked at the pit:

Foreshift 1.30 am.

To tell you the truth it's a bit of a relief to shut that door behind my Ralphy and his uncle Jonna. Those men-folk had a clean go of it. All they had to do was get themselves out to work. Their pit clothes were brushed and ready, clean work socks hanging on the rail above the fireplace, their boots brushed clean and dry on the hearth. I'd put up their baits and filled their tin bottles with cold tea before they got up. And no matter what the shift I like them to go off with sommat inside them, even if it's only hot tea and dripping and bread. Today, though, it was good pork-dripping from Frankie Cornish's pig. He's not a bad lad, that Frankie. He always says fair shares for all, specially so in these hard times. It's hard enough for us, with our men who are actually in work. It's harder still for those who have no jobs, and there's plenty of them about.

Once I've shut the door behind them I rake down the fire and give it a bit of a poke to liven it up. Then I throw on a bucket of coal and draw the coals across to the boiler side. There's an art to it, dealing with this range of mine especially for baking and especially today, it being wash-day. Wash-day takes gallons of water, hot and cold. It's gunna be a really busy day. *Gird up your loins*. It says that in the Bible but I think that referred to a battle. Wash-day is battle enough for me or any woman.

Now, though, there's a moment of quiet here in the lamplight. Not a sound anywhere. So I sit down at the table and pour myself the last cup from the pot. I scrape the last of the dripping over the last slice of bread and enjoy a bite myself. Only one loaf left. Not much chance to bake today, all the fire used up, like, to heat the hot water. So I'll send one of the young'n's down to the shop for a loaf. Mebbe not, though. My Ralphy doesn't like shop bread. Mebbe I'll get a couple of loaves in when the washing's done. It's hard working from one fire, like …

My mother Barbara's view, of course, contradicted the well deserved high esteem in which pitmen were viewed generally. The truth is, they weren't all confined to the macho stereotype. Some of them were great family men, great sportsmen, committed politicians, they could be intellectual, perceptive, artistic, poetic. I think of the writing of Sid Chaplin, whose novel *The Thin Seam* I consider outstanding. Then there are the Ashington Painters – working miners whose paintings are now so well curated in the Woodhorn Museum. My own area rejoices in the gifted visualisation of pit culture by Norman Cornish and the great art of Tom McGuinness - a modest man who broke away from merely depicting this life into expressing it in universal terms. His dark brooding prints sit on my study walls and are always an inspiration when, in my fiction, I want to venture into that arcane underground world.

From *Where Hope Lives* (2001). Gabriel is a young pitman in the 1930s, a talented painter who has been encouraged by the leader of The Settlement, set up to cultivate the artistic skills among pitmen, employed and unemployed:

I close my eyes against the dark and listen to the murmuring in the gallery. Tegger's shoulder lies heavy against mine and I know he's having his five minute nap to keep him going for the rest of his shift. I close my own eyes. Around me the gallery stills…

I open my eyes, blinking. The pit face before me is gleaming with a strange light, the dark behind it threaded with shards of silver. I lean across to feel my lamp but it's still on the *Off* position. I look back at the old coal face and the gleam is still there. Phosphorous! I've heard about it in old pitmen's tales. But the gleam's too great for phosphorous. The hair on the back of my neck prickles and I scramble to light my lamp. My gob of light throws itself into the black chasm, chasing away the luminescent glow. But now there's a figure. I screw up my eyes to see it more clearly. Is it another man moving in the dark to relieve himself? A pony on the wander? Worse has been known.

But it's not a man. It's a woman with a shadowy face, her dark clothes only relieved by a glittering red patch on her shoulder. A flower maybe. Or blood.

… Answers flow into my head, through my veins. This is more than any of that. It's the earth herself enfolding us in work and sleep. She forgives us our gouging, our cutting and harvesting and reclaims us for her own. With our blind wonder, our sparkle of imagined colour, with our helpless charging and working of the depths, we are her unborn children to be born again into the bright world at the end of each shift. And then, at the beginning of the next shift we're sucked back into her overwhelming void as the cage drops yet again and spews us into the galleries which are the wounds we cut into her side…

The Psychic

We only found out in the 1980s that my mother's father Tom Blair had married someone else - a woman called Lily, who died - before he married Sarah Ellen. (Yet *another* secret in this family). Auntie Lily, the eldest – and most eccentric – of my aunts, was obviously called after her. This aunt, like Barbara, lived away from her home town most of her life and was also marked out as different. Like the others though, she had good hands: she made lace and was an exquisite embroiderer. But she also smoked Capstan double strength and drank Guinness, which was a mark against her in their Methodist eyes. She had a hoarse voice, talked with a Yorkshire accent and died at fifty two from a chest infection.

In Bradford, where she lived most of her adult life, she sometimes acted as an advocate for post-war stateless refugees. In her boarding house I met interesting, even exotic, displaced Poles and Latvians. One outcome of this for me is that, eventually, a series of Polish characters have emerged in my novels. It seems they were there, sitting in my subconscious, waiting to be called out from Auntie Lily's life in the 1950s.

Picture This: The girl is eight. She's not feeling very pretty now. She feels sad and lost. In the chaos and uncertainty after her father dies she's been sent, with her more confident and competent sister, to her Auntie Lily's home in Bradford. The house is full of men, brawny, loud people, unlike her lost Daddy, There are some, though, that have fine features and foreign accents. There is one beautiful, pale lady who wanders around the house. Her strange language, gargled back in her throat, fascinates the girl. One day a policeman comes to the door and our girl follows her Auntie Lily and one of the lodgers out onto the street. The pale lady is dancing on the corner dressed only in a green nightie. She starts, screams, and bolts. They all give chase, the little girl among them. The lady stops at the foot of some kind of monument, shivering. They move to surround her. Auntie Lily takes her hand. The policeman takes her arm on the other side. Silence reigns, broken only by the scream of an ambulance siren. The lady's wild, frightened eyes meet those of the little girl whom she recognises as a fellow lost soul.

From *No Rest for The Wicked* (2005)
In Paris 1923, on the day of the funeral of Sarah Bernhardt, young Pippa is returning with bread to Palmer's Varieties - her English Theatre Troup - when she comes upon a strange scene in a back street:

> ... all these people – poor working people by their dress – were staring goggle-eyed at a young woman who was whirling and dancing in the narrow alleyway. She wore no shift beneath her long gown and her limbs gleamed under the sheer, green fabric. The bright shade of her dress was reflected in the dozens of ragged ribbons tied anyhow in her hair. As the woman danced her tapestry sack bag moved softly against her body...

Auntie Lily, like my character Stella in *An Englishwoman in France*, was gifted with second sight. I remember being thrilled once when I saw my aunt calling up the dead in a Spiritualist Church in my home town, on one of her visits from Bradford. She was very convincing, telling people their own stories - she clearly knew what they wanted to hear.

There are sensitive people, with intuition - even second sight - in many of my novels but for the first time in what I call 'my French novel' *An Englishwoman in France*, I've embraced these ideas as a fundamental part of my central character Stella, a professional astrologer with a gift of her own..

The minute you enter these ideas of seeing through time, talking to people from the past, many people – anxious editors amongst them - throw up their hands and become abnormally nervous. The paradox is that novels that involve much more extreme aspects of the para-normal ride high in the charts of best-selling books.

I try to explain that researching novels can lead you down strange pathways. Star signs? All nonsense of course. But which of us does not have the desire for some shape, some purpose in the randomised pick-and-mix of human experience? Of course we can discover purposeful shape in the certainties of organised religion or the world of science and the academy.

I have this friend who doesn't believe in any of the metaphysical explanations. He thinks there's something more than coincidence behind coincidences. We talk about CJ Jung and his ideas of *synchronicity* and the *conscience collective* – a kind of well of human experience, wisdom and perception which - some say now - may be genetically accumulated. I suppose my own accumulated wisdom, perception and unique experience come from all the elements I've described here in *The Romancer* and are sprinkled like the glittering shards of a kaleidoscope throughout my stories. In my stories I make my own patterns of understanding.

So far, so unscientific!

Despite this lack of science we do seem to need this reassurance of greater patterns; some order to life before and after death. Look at the way some unscientific folk embrace the work of Einstein, Schrödinger and others, who have challenged the notion of a linear time, suggesting a warping, bending, reversing, and even breaking of the received wisdom of time's straight arrow, arguing their corner by means of the mechanisms of relativity and quantum physics.

Emerging from the womb, we encounter a world of blooming, buzzing confusion and start to seek out patterns that will explain it all. Religions of every sort - including the schools of scientific theory and academic precepts – flaunt their holy books, their heroes and their villains and offer us this seductive comfort: if we follow *their* rules they will make shapely sense for us, rescuing us from our individual blooming buzzing confusion.

The old habit of reading the stars in the night sky and interpreting them to ascribe character and to predict the future - *if time's not linear then the future is there to see!* - is the most immediate and possibly the most primitive of these processes. And like many people, over my morning coffee, I read my stars in newspapers and magazines. This notion of restorative magic has engendered parallel professions – astrologers, hypnotists, gurus; there are even people out there – ordinary nuts-and-bolts people whom I've met – who call themselves *shamans*.

A secret vice of mine is to check out personality types designated by the stars. I am Pisces -' *impressionable, compassionate, sensitive, artistic, mystical, meditative, spiritual, a medium, also escapist - tendency to flight, dependent , masochistic. Can be mendacious* (ie tendency to tell lies – come to think of it I *tell lies* - ie stories - for a living!) And *paranoid,* (eg Why is nobody in Germany reading my wonderful stories?)

I have to tell you that, in my case, all these aspects of personality are more or less true. I do have dozens of other characteristics but even these link back to those qualities one way or another.

Looking at other Pisceans I can see these qualities coming through in them - lots of actors; many writers; politicians; inventors and thinkers (including the afore-mentioned Albert Einstein). I imagine as well that prisons and psychiatric units will have their fair share of rather more anonymous Pisceans, with their mendacity, paranoia and desire to escape.

Talking of prisons - which interest me as you will see - the joint star sign of the Kray Twins (see my novel *The Lavender House*) was Scorpio '*resourcefulness, penetrating insight, strength in crisis, psychic power, charisma, strong sexuality, interest in occult, secretiveness, jealousy.'* This case illustrates that given characteristics are not value-free. They can be turned on their heads and applied with death-dealing negativity.

From ***An Englishwoman in France** (2011)* The astrologer Estella is in France recovering from the murder of her daughter Siri. She is staying at the *Maison d'Estella:*

.... I get up and poke around among my stuff in the room.
But still I can't settle. So I climb up the narrow wooden

staircase to the roof and lie down on the Lilo that lives up there. I can smell Mae's sun lotion. The night is warm, the sky is dark. I take a very deep breath, pleased to be here along with the sky.

Then I can hear footsteps coming up the wooden staircase and I feel a prickle of distaste, thinking Philip will spoil this experience, spoil it, I know he will!

It's not Philip. It's young Olga. Silently she comes and lies alongside me.

I take another very deep breath.

Olga takes her own deep, noisy breath. 'What are we doing, Auntie Stella?'

'We're looking for Virgo. See! Those nine stars? One, two, three, four, five, six, seven, eight, and see that one on the end. Nine.'

Her chuckle warms the air between us. 'I see it! Like a little handbag in the sky. It's really pretty.'

'So it is.'

'What does it mean, the little handbag?'

'It means a lot of things to a lot of people.'

'What does it mean to you?'

'It means a person I once knew.'

'Which person?'

I hesitate. 'A girl called Siri.'

She lies very still, absorbing that. 'And is it her handbag, with her special things in it?'

'I hope so.'

Then her small white hand raises itself and points at another constellation. 'And what is that one? That big pointy one?'

'Ursa Major. But we call it the Great Bear.'

She chuckles. 'I can see him! I can see his toes and

his long tail. 'Who does he make you think of?'

I wait a moment. In the years since Siri was taken I've avoided thinking of him, avoided thinking that if I'd gone after him with news of her, if I'd broken his family and made him mine, Siri would still be here. Now I'm thinking about him and that night in the Deer House. 'I haven't thought of him for a long time,' I say carefully. 'It's a man called Ludovic.'

'Is he nice?' she says. 'Is he as nice as my Daddy?'

'I think he might be. But I don't know him very well.'

Then minutes pass and there's silence beside me. My eye returns to Virgo and I project my mind, my heart, to that small handbag in the sky. Siri is near. It's funny about Siri being Virgo. Our signs are very incompatible but she's part of me and I am part of her. Another thing that puts the whole theory in flight, you might say.

Rings ... Romance

Last year I forgot my wedding anniversary. What's more, *he* forgot too! We fell into each other's arms and laughed, concluding that living the life meant more than cards and flowers. There was some talk of long service medals, however.

This is a marriage that went to work and loved it, that had flowers in its hair, that wore sober suits and hippy skirts. It walked children in second-hand prams, and sat in cafes writing while they rolled round the floor. It went to PTA meetings. It took holidays by the seaside that needed two ponchos to keep warm. It went to the races, to rugby matches and to school plays. It waved off children to their new life and welcomed them back again. It watched cricket and football and cop shows on TV. It read newspapers at length. It read books and wrote them. And it delivered heavy manuscripts to the Post Office. It visited clinics and hospitals and held its breath. It's a marriage that travels and continues to relish the youngest, the boy who loves chocolate. It's a marriage that still holds hands.

Once, when we'd been married for about six years (still very young...) I went to the school where I worked without my wedding ring, having left it in the bathroom. A woman colleague shuddered at the sight of my naked finger, saying, 'I couldn't do that, leave my ring off. I'd feel as though I didn't belong to my husband.'

I thought about this and decided that I'd never felt as though I *belonged* to anyone. In fact, growing up had – for me - been the process of establishing just that fact. So, for the next ten years I wore no ring at all, thinking people had to get to know me without the ring-label. I didn't want people to have rigid expectations of me, especially the expectation that I *belonged* to someone.

Then, when I felt I'd made my point, I wore a ring again. In fact, in the end, I wore two.

These were the decades when *Romance* and the quest of *belonging* to or owning someone were rife. We'd never had it so good and one symbol of this was the chronic absorption in the notion of romance. Romance was the big selling point for films, books, magazines and advertisements for perfume, soap and Martinis. Novels published by Mills & Boon - and their more pretentious imitators - steepled into millions.

Bridget Jones, following the more elegant Jane Austen, disguised her quest with suitable irony but *Romance* and *Lifelong Love* are there in the subtext of the Bridget Jones novel, like Blackpool printed through a stick of rock. These days chick-lit and mum-lit novels and derivative films - for all their savvy street style – rehearse the same blind and bland quest for Romance, although the *lifelong* bit may have slipped a bit.

The pity is that none of us or our lives can measure up to the Romance, to the glamorous puppetry of such fictions. In fact there's a yawning gap between these polished creatures and the chunky ill-shapen bodies, mussed up hair and the harassed lives of both women and men in real life. The billion-pound glamour industry in all its forms promotes itself very nicely into this gap, thank you. The cosmetic surgery industry imposes on society many tight-faced male and female ghosts of Dorian Gray

It's a good thing then, that despite our lack of glamour, so many of us rejoice in long term relationships that evolve and develop through the years – larger this year, narrower next; disappointments this year, surprises next. Living here. Living there. Jobs gained. Jobs lost. Clinging together. Mourning together. Running away. Coming back. Making time for yourself. Arguing your corner. Holding hands.

This life is neither film nor fantasising storybook; it's no jolly idyll that leaps from passion to perfect parenthood, to empty-nest-adventure. It's a bumpier - but much more exciting - ride than that. What it is, is two separate people making it up as they go along, becoming lifetime comrades and mutually appreciative buddies in a relationship that continues to change, evolve, soften, sharpen, as the years go by. A sophisticated romance, you might say.

I mentioned here that these days I rejoice in wearing two rings on my wedding finger. The second one is from my mother Barbara. She wore it for the short fifteen years of her happily married life and for the thirty six years of her not so happy widowhood. I'm touched and honoured to wear it.

Perhaps I should have another ring – a kind of long service medal. I'd buy *him* one, but he'd never wear it. He's never believed in men wearing rings and sticks to his view.

From the short story, ***Married Life?*** from my collection ***Knives*** *(2009)* Not autobiographical, this *is* a forensic, possibly comic, examination of the long marriage between Imogen and her husband Freddie. Submissive wife Imogen has finally broken out, visited India and made new lifelong friends:

> …Imogen's new friends considered her very special and treated her tenderly. After six weeks she came back with a notebook full of contact addresses all over the world and some wonderful photographs. Freddie barely glanced at them. He was not interested in these wonders. After all he had not been there. And anyway he'd just acquired a first edition R C Hutchinson in an Edinburgh Oxfam shop. He gloated about it to Imogen. Now that he had every edition of every one of Hutchinson's masterpieces, he could relax…

The Holocaust Survivor
and the Little Children

There are some stories that you can't improve on, even in fiction. Like many who grew up in those years after the Second World War, the events and outcomes of that war are hard-wired into my intellectual system, providing markers for the nature of virtue and evil that survive in me to this day. Inevitably, like many writers of my generation, war creeps into my fiction.

After the Second World War my childish mind grappled helplessly with reportage of the terrible acts that could only be called evil. Later in my life I read and studied more about the war and was able to contextualise, if not bury, such horrors. This year is the seventieth anniversary of the Blitz and yet again the newspapers and media are full of that war. But somehow, a quaintness is emerging, a distance that renders these events in the sepia shades of the English Civil War or the French Revolution.

But for some people it is all too real. In 2009 I chaired an event at a library near here, between eighty-seven year old Sylvia Hurst and a large group of child and adult readers. Sylvia was there to talk about her autobiography *Laugh or Cry,* in which she tells of her life in Germany before and after she escaped the Holocaust seventy years before, in 1939.

The children of Ox Close School – bright faced and interested - reminded me of myself at that age. Bizarrely, it was Red Nose Day, so they streamed into the Library in fancy dress, red and green hair, sporting painted faces. Some girls wore party dresses and pyjamas. Some boys came in football shirts. They, with a sprinkling of adults, were there to meet Sylvia Hurst, *née* Fleischer, who as a young girl, escaped Nazi Germany on the last train - the *kindertransport* – sent by their families to safety in England as the war clouds were gathering.

The children sat on mats in orderly rows and listened as Sylvia spoke eloquently of her happy pre-war life as a member of the loving family of an affluent corset maker, who so believed in Germany that he refused to leave. In the end, like his wife - Sylvia's mother who loved *haute couture* – he died with other members of the family, in extermination camps. Richard, Sylvia's younger, thirteen year old brother, had also stayed behind. Mr Fleischer thought the *kindertransport* would be too dangerous for him. Richard was taken by the Nazis but survived the camp to which he was sent. Sylvia told the children, 'You know, those living skeletons you see in the pictures? My little brother Richard was one of those at the end.'

But, she, reassured them - in his eighties now - Richard still lives in America and has had a long and fulfilled life.

Sylvia, at sixteen, was really too old for the *kindertransport*, but had been appointed to escort younger children to a certain station, and by some blessed error, was allowed to continue. After a hard journey Sylvia arrived in England where - her pristine German sense of cleanliness offended - she first lived in a flea-ridden house in the East End. Then she went to live with rather reluctant relatives and to work in their factory. Later, she went on to be a successful West End dressmaker and designer, then on to lecture in Manchester on fashion design. Finally, finally, she moved up to Tantobie in County Durham, where she ran her own pub and well-known restaurant.

Sylvia sat there in the library so full of energy, occasionally bursting into laughter as she told her tale. She had combed her once-blonde, now grey curls down over her shoulders because – she told me - she thought the children would like it that way, would see her as a heroine or a princess...

Still, you might think this was heavy duty material for ten year olds. But these children had been prepared by their teachers, had read appropriate material and had visited an Ann Frank exhibition that was touring at the time. (I have to admit I have to stifle a thought that the horrors of the Holocaust had been inappropriately tamed by being 'on the curriculum'. I also had to stifle my distaste in Cracow - researching *The Woman Who Drew Buildings* - at the sight of colourful jaunting cars advertising trips to Auschwitz.)

But the children here asked wonderfully searching and insightful questions, drawing even more extraordinary information from this unique lady. Subjects ranged from brainwashing, to *haute couture*, to the kind of things Sylvia had chosen to put into the single suitcase she was allowed to take on the train. (Her father had said she could choose any suitcase to take with her. She chose a fine crocodile skin case, which she later regretted because it was so heavy.) For me, the best question was the little girl who asked what *it felt like*, to go through all this.

So Sylvia Hurst, in her still strongly accented English, described again the joys of secure family life in pre-war Germany being shattered by inhuman, shameful events that no child – no person – should endure. As she spoke she used examples from the children's own world, here and now, to illustrate her loss and her suffering as a child.

It felt to me like magic, then, as these children used their considerable imaginations to enter the world of this lady - seventy six years their senior – and grasped something of her extraordinary life. They transformed their technical understanding of a bit of the 'history curriculum' into genuine empathy with someone who had lived it.

In the tea break that followed, one by one, the children came up and cuddled this old lady, almost as though to comfort the little girl - not much older than them - who had been left alone and had lost her family in the Holocaust.

I must say that no novel, however exquisitely written, could aspire to evoke the empathy inspired by this true story.

Adventurers All

I suppose as writers and readers we're all armchair adventurers, whether it's into the darker regions of our own and others' psyche, or to the far corners of the earth. One of my armchair heroines has always been Elizabeth David, whose graceful writing and transforming knowledge of the importance of food and taste also expresses a swashbuckling nature and a delicious devil-may-care attitude to convention. She transformed attitudes to food in Britain after the parched years of the Second World War. Her most engaging adventure for me was sailing with a lover from Britain right down through the French rivers and canals to the Mediterranean in 1939, (cooking all the way, of course …) only to be arrested and held for a while by the Italians as an enemy alien.

Like the story of Sylvia Hurst and the *Kindertransport,* another inspiring story where the truth is stranger and stronger than fiction, I am fascinated by that of Nira and Allan Chidgey whom I met by the accident of renting their house in Agde in the Languedoc.

Allan and Nira now live just by the river Hérault, in an exquisite house whose terrace is like a ship's prow. Allan is English, a painter by profession, and a seafarer by preference. Nira is Israeli, the daughter of a silversmith and was once a restorer of ceramics. These two met in London in the 1980s when they were both living on boats on the Thames. Allan was painting, and very much into buying boats and sailing. He went to Amsterdam, bought a decommissioned barge, rebuilt it entirely as a sailing barge, then, with Nira, sailed it across the channel and down the rivers and canals of France right as far as the Mediterranean at the port of Agde. I like to compare their story to that of Elizabeth David.

Allan and Nira had never heard of Agde but on that journey, sailing down to the Camargue they stopped in Agde to buy film, fell in love with this ancient city 'that time had forgot' and settled They eventually applied their amazing boat-restoring and design skills to restoring, among others, the lovely old house the Maison d'Estella where I stay.

This house is the inspiration, of course, for *An Englishwoman in France*. From the first time I saw it I had this weird feeling that I knew this place, that I'd been here before. And so the writing, the chapters, started to unfold in my head and onto the notebooks. I felt there had to be someone here who could see – even move - through time into the layers of the old city. And so the astrologer Stella walks into the story, into this house, to regain her sanity after the insanity of the murder of her daughter. She drops through time to meet the boy who will eventually be martyred and become St Thibery, the patron saint of the mentally ill.

Writing the early chapters actually in the house I became absorbed in legends and stories that have survived around this place for more that a thousand years. One story that really engaged me was about a time after the death of Jesus, when a boat landed here on this coast with a precious cargo. This cargo is variously described as *Three Marys* – Magdalene, Jacobé, Salomé - as well as their dark Egyptian maid Sarah (later adopted by the Gitan/Roma as their own Saint); possibly also a grail or container of some sort; possibly the bones of Jesus the Nazarene; possibly Jesus himself, in the flesh, alive, ready to conquer Europe with love…

Allan and Nira brought up two children (now grownup) in the house and it has the feeling of a house with a very personal continuous history. This house itself is at least four hundred years old and there were houses here before that – not least, I worked out, the house of the Roman Governor of Agde, who had a son called Thibery who was, eventually, the Christian saint. It's position, high on the ridge (still called *la rue Haute*), had a sweeping view of the port and the Mediterranean. So I felt – *knew* – that there had been people living in a house on the ridge is since the Greeks were here in 600 BC. The Greeks, then the Romans, and a sprinkling of pirates, all arrived here as seafarers - adventurers all, like Elizabeth David. And like Allan and Nira Chidgey.

From *An Englishwoman in France*: *(2011)* Stella and Richard arrive at the house:
     ….Instead, we were making our way to a bulky house
     behind a high black-stone wall, with a massive door that

looked as if it had been hammered by the mailed fist of Richard the Lionheart. I looked along the narrow street and shivered. The high wall was pierced with smaller doors and other windows, which seemed to have been carved into the walls with a random hand. But I knew this doorway on the high ridge of the town had at one time been an important place. In my mind's eye I could see a great arch and an eagle.

The door creaked open onto an irregular courtyard set around by windows and walls that rose up into a bowl, cradling the blue southern sky. To one side was a stone balustered staircase that led to a blocked off doorway, going nowhere. Seagulls chirped, chattered, shrieked in French and posed on the topmost ramparts.

I breathed in deeply.

The place smelled of time, of layers of life and people. Around me the deserted courtyard tumbled with a whirling smoke of people going about their eternal business of survival, commerce and politics. Their gauzy layers welcomed me. I breathed out. For the first time in months - in years now, I felt comfortable.

A leaflet on the old heavy table in the big kitchen informed us that the stones on the boundary wall of our house were part of the ancient town wall, built, like many buildings here, in pockmarked black volcanic stone, quarried throughout the millennia from the slopes of an ancient volcano.

Philip turned to me. 'No beach then!' he said, making every effort to be cheerful.

The Gift of the Exceptional Mary D

My novel ***The Woman Who Drew Buildings*** is dedicated : '*For the exceptional and inspirational Mary Davies - painter, writer and healer.*'

I met Mary Davies – then in her early eighties - at a workshop I ran in Cumbria. Half as old again as other participants she was a youthful inspiration to the group - a delight to work with. A believer in reincarnation, Mary had already written a book about her various incarnations through time and had brought with her a half-finished novel set in the 1960s. We became friends. I visited her on the isle of Arran where she lives and she came down into England – boat-train-train-train to visit me for two book launches. In time she published two of her own novels in good editions which sold in great numbers. As well as this she continued to paint, relishing the shore-side view from her window. On one of my visits to the island she showed me her straw coffin, standing up in one corner, used for occasional storage. It was very colourful. She'd had a party with her friends and they all contributed their own decoration.

Mary had trained as an artist and had moved into the civil service in the field of buildings conservation. She reported and wrote for the eminent buildings historian Niklaus Pevsner. She had married late and very happily to a fellow Quaker and had ten good years before he died.

One of the stories she told me was about visiting Poland to document buildings at a time when it was very restricted by Soviet domination in the 1980s. She lived for weeks at a time just as the Polish themselves did, under very difficult conditions. One day, coming to join me for a book launch, she arrived laden with a big box a box of materials about her travels and experience in Poland in the 1980s. There were photographs, pamphlets, tickets, brochures, wonderful diaries as well as her own drawings.

Mary knew I was interested in the idiosyncrasies of letters, notebooks, images and ephemera that I used to inspire and to inject real life into my novels. I was, she said, to use them as I wished. We had long talks about her experiences and the dilemma of using them as inspiration, for what I knew would be pure fiction.

After that it took me some years to develop my imaginative take on all this material and all these ideas, in order to allow the novel to emerge of its own volition. It became more fluid – easier to write - when my purely imagined characters got to grips with the material emerging from Mary's boxes.

I kept saying to Mary I would *not* write her life story, as interesting as it might be. But she kept saying, 'You are to do as you wish with the materials, dear.'

My problem was how to pay proper respect to Mary's own wonderful spirit, while holding to myself the right to write fiction. I needed a mechanism to make this distinction clear. In the end –as often happens – I found the answer in that moment between sleeping and waking. I had a half-dream of a boy trudging down from the railway station in Durham City. I felt he was a clever boy, but was just out of prison. I knew this was the beginning of the novel.

This changed the fictional dynamics emerging from Mary's factual material. I knew that here was my answer. Mary Davies had no children but I knew this boy was the son of the fictional Marie Mathève who, like my Mary, went to Poland to look at and draw buildings in the 1980s. Marie Mathève contains the spirit of my Mary Davies but had her own entirely fictional life.

I was on real tenterhooks when the novel was published, at the thought of Mary reading it. I was relieved to know that she loved it, and read it twice straight off. She told me that it made her relive those amazing days. I breathed a sigh of creative relief.

From *The Woman Who Drew Buildings* (2009):

With the Zielinskis In Chorzow,1981

....Marie fingered her face to see if it was still there. Her cheek was cold as ice. She rubbed it hard to unfreeze it, then tucked her hand back under the clothes to warm it up again. She was warm enough from the neck down: the heap of woven blankets saw to that. She lifted her head slightly to see through the gap in the meagre curtains. At home, when it was this cold, the glass would be etched with butterflies, steeples and mountains of frost. This had always seemed like magic to her, making up for the cold which she so disliked. But the glass in these windows was quite clear. They have double or even triple glazing perhaps. Despite their grim aspect, these were modern buildings. But, as far as she could tell at this moment, they were entirely without heat.

From the next room Marie could hear the clatter of dishes and movement: murmuring voices, the piping call of a child, the soothing tone of a mother, then the sound of harpsichord music which changed suddenly to spitting-out military music, interspersed with urgent words that she could not understand. She lay back, closed her eyes and considered her dilemma. What on earth was she doing here up on the eighth floor, taking up almost half the available space in a freezing flat that was barely big enough for two, but which housed five, now six with herself?

Such proximity! She was not used to being this close to anyone. Her house on the new estate - hers since her mother died - was sprawling compared with this. She loved her house. Everything there – the glass fronted bookshelves, the huge architect's work table in the dining room – was dedicated to her love for, her obsession with, architecture. She'd always counted herself lucky to live alone, so she could concentrate on writing her reports on the precious buildings, streets, bridges and warehouses that were in danger. It was worth taking care with the reports. She sometimes felt ashamed of her vanity but she knew her work made a difference: buildings and streets had survived because of her intervention.

Charisma and Café Writing

I relish the fact that writer Natalie Goldberg and my late, great, very lamented, friend Julia Darling have both, in their times, been great advocates of writing in cafes.

While I was in Agde in France I posted on my blog a eulogistic piece about scribbling in the Cafe Plazza and the cafe on *la Place de La Marine*. In fact my delight in getting away from the desk, out into the street, into the inspiring neutrality of a cafe did not start in France at all. It is an old, almost lifelong habit that I found I shared with Julia Darling.

Julia was charismatic, not just a great tutor, poet and playwright, she was a novelist and lyrical poet who wrung every last drop of joy and delight, love and affection, out of her writer's life, before her tragically early death.

For several years she came here to give wildly popular workshops on her own and sometimes alongside me. We talked more than once of collaborating on publishing a Writing Workshop book. But time ran out. Despite her great gifts she was modest and comradely - as well as merry, enabling and respectful of others' talent. She always worked alongside the writing work-shoppers, never sat on a pedestal above them. She risked herself alongside them in the read-around, saying, 'Well this is mad, but...'

Julia was the mistress of original, telling, firecracker metaphors and knew the magic of the right word in the right place. Our work-shoppers would go off inspired to write closer, to do better.

When lunchtime came around she'd rush off, either to swim, or go to a greasy spoon cafe near the old Post Office. She did this for rest, for refreshment, and inevitably, for inspiration from the other tables, where bin men and office workers would stoke themselves up with cake or a good fry-up for the afternoon's work. Things overheard there would be filed away in that considerable intelligence and become a natural resource for her in her writing. She had a sympathetic and an empathetic ear for the natural dialogue of so-called ordinary people.

This is interesting, as although she was a bit of a maverick, she came from a distinctive upper class intellectual background. But she was uniquely classless in her apprehension of the life and people around her - so very refreshing in writing circles, which can be riddled with all kinds of ridiculous snobbery.

Much has been made of the graceful and poetic way in which Julia tackled the process of dying - writing on her blog of its challenges with frighteningly forensic insight and luminous grace. To be honest, though, I prefer to think of her in terms of the way she lived. She was a joy to be with, wryly witty and always kind. She was inspirational and prepared to be inspired. She lit up any room she was in with her broad smile and wide eyes.

In my own cafe sojourns eavesdropping is of secondary importance to a clear table not far from the window and staff who will both take care of me and ignore me. Mostly I sit there and fill my diary with plans; make both creative and practical lists; draft posts for my blog. In France I would scribble the next chapter for *An Englishwoman in France* and read a heavy tome about 'Gaul in Antiquity'. (More interesting than it sounds…)

These times away from the desk are essential for someone who works from home. Surrounded by strangers, I work very quickly, get a great deal done. This book, *The Romancer,* has been partly drafted in the orangery of The Whitworth Hotel, in an idyllic setting quite near to me. I wrote almost the whole of my novel *Honesty's Daughter* here. That novel is set here, in what used to be the house of the Shafto family, whose famous son Bobby went to sea, *'a silver buckle on his knee.'*

Yesterday as I was walking to a high street cafe I passed two men talking. One man was saying to the other. '…and as well as that I've got this cancer ripping away at my insides…' This so perfectly expressed a combination of anger and stoicism that it made me want to cry.

And it made me think again about the radiant, charismatic Julia Darling.

From *An Englishwoman in France (2011)*:

...The images whirl together, the clatter and noise swells and recedes in my ears. Then I notice an old woman sitting at a table in front of me, a straw boater planted straight on top of an grey-blonde pony tail and wearing neat blue jeans and a battered white linen jacket. She is pointing to a little white Sheltie dog beside her feet. I can't hear her words but she's pointing at the dog, chastising him in the fashion people use with dogs when they don't really mean it.

He ignores her, wanders across and lifts his storybook face up to look at me. I've no idea what you do with a dog. I lean down and scratch his neck. 'Now then, doggie!' I say, my own ridiculous statement ringing in my ears.

The old woman catches my glance and smiles. 'English?' she says.

I nod and smile back. She's harder to read. Her neatness, her composure, her nut brown skin are distinctly un-English. *'Et vous?'* I say.

'I am English also.' She allows a trill of laughter to escape her small neat mouth. 'But in France forty years now so I sound neither one nor the other.'

'Forty years?' It's been so long since I've been curious about any stranger.

'I came here to Paris to demonstrate with the students in sixty eight and never managed to leave, I'm afraid.' She's right about her accent. It *is* neither one thing nor another.

'But you live here in Agde? A long way from Paris.'

She nods. 'Is a long story. After the demonstrations I

sailed down here on the rivers and canals with two of my new friends. I married one of them and he was a *professeur* here at the *Lycée* for many years. So I stayed and taught here as well.' She shrugged. '*Hélas,* he is gone now, my Ettienne. But we were long together.'

Her sadness worries me. I look through the café crowd at the square with its statue and its fountain glittering in the sun, 'This is a very mysterious place,' I find myself saying.

She smiles encouragingly. 'Ah, you see this? Everyone does not see it. Agde is a place of all the ages. Do you know that they are digging down at the quay just now? And there is this big hole and you can see five cities layered down there, one on top of the other. You can see the layer of charred wood where the Spanish – I think it was the Spanish – burned the town. All time is here, dear, right back to six hundred years before even Christ walked the earth...'

Global Interests
& Travelling in the Head

One of the nicest things in my house is a good sized globe of the world. This globe is very tactile, with the mountains and high lands of the world in high relief. It's very good for letting your fingers do the walking.

In the less privileged house of my childhood we just had this big book, this battered atlas of the world. We children used to pore over it with my mother Barbara, as she traced the routes of the explorers Magellan and Vasco da Gama, Cristoforo Columbus and Sebastian Cabot, Drake and Raleigh, Scott and Shackleton. And now, going back, I would add Elizabeth David and Nira and Allan Chidgey, and my fictional old woman and her husband Ettienne.

I look at my globe, seeing again just where the Hérault meets the Mediterranean and how far it is from Israel and the Middle East. I imagine what distances really meant in other times, without the power of steam, internal combustion engines and the jet planes. My finger traces other routes as I think of the other places my own modern family has travelled, in the more modern way – Australia, New Zealand, Singapore, Jamaica, Grenada, Boston USA, China, Africa and Indonesia.

Researching the nature of travel in the early centuries after the death of Christ for *An Englishwoman in France*, I find myself blinking at the thousands of miles St Paul walked in the countries of the Eastern Mediterranean travelling on, alongside, or behind, a donkey. I blanch at the death toll involved in travelling by sea, and understand for the first time the sailors' need to keep in sight of land for fear of shipwreck, pirates and vengeful weather.

Looking again at the old maps I imagine the difficulty of the Three Marys' journey from Galilee to Gaul with their precious and iconic burden, whatever that might be. (Just imagining what this burden might be has been part of the work of thinking about for this novel.)

I locate the site of Nicodemia, East of Istanbul, just between the Aegean Sea and the Black Sea, where the Roman Emperor Diocletian built a city and located his court for a time. Now I have to imagine just how my three characters can make the journey from Gaul to Nicodemia in 303AD without falling off the edge of the world and out of my novel.

This *travelling in the head* is a family tradition. In reality poverty meant that mother never travelled – not even to London - until she was fifty two. But when she was fifty two she went alone by boat across the River Tyne for a week in Denmark and her real travels – outside her head - began. But as a child I learned from her the adventure of *travelling in the head,* which is such a great resource for a writer.

I had to confine myself to *travelling in the head* until I was thirty two years old, when I went to Paris, to the Sèvres factory, for an education conference. Although I'd learned French with the fantastic Mr Phorson for seven years, had read poetry and novels in French with robust appreciation, and loved French history and culture, I'd never set foot in the country to hear the language in its own habitat.

Since then I've travelled and stayed in various parts of France but it was only in recent years, when I landed in the Languedoc, in the city of Agde, that I felt at home. And in this part of France the French is either strongly accented or not French at all – as different from French as Gaelic is from English.

In my story, in that first century at least, this Gaullish coast might have seemed to be a place of greater safety for the Nazarene travellers. Unlike people in other parts of the Roman Empire, the Gauls (like the British) even though still under the sway of pagan Rome, disliked the growing official emperor-cult. I came to see that after their long sea journey these Nazarene visitors might be comforted by some similarities of life here on the coast of Gaul, with their lives by the sea of Galilee: shouting sailors, milling fishing boats, women sorting fish, men hauling nets or mending them as they watched the river and considered the wind and the conditions.

I can see scenes like this even in our modern time.

Towns along this coast abound with stories of these women - from St Marie de la Mère, to Rennes le Chateau - all share elements of these legends. Agde has its own Mary story – the little village close by here celebrates a vision of the Virgin Mary whose prayers saved the city from the flooding by the River Hérault. Apparently the rock on which a hermit had a vision of her kneeling and bidding the waters to recede, has marks of her knees. This is an important generic story around the city of Agde. Here at the mouth of the River Hérault the fear of flood – *l'inondation* - is no mere legend. The town has been seriously flooded here more than once in living memory. The fear is very real. That miraculous image of the flood receding and people being saved must inhabit many people's dreams.

Picture this: Our girl is much, much older now: she's a long term writer always restless for new ideas. She loves this city and is invaded by a sense that she's been here before. She knows the layers of time in this ancient place. One night, sleeping in this old house in the bed shaped like a boat she has a dream. She sees four cloaked women huddled together on a quayside, where ships are massed like herringbones stitched to the stone wall with clanking iron chains. The women mutter to each other wondering what to do next, in their quest for protection and safety. They glance back at two men, standing a respectful distance: one is a brother, the other is big- shouldered, used to digging gardens. In her dream she knows this man is stricken that his garden was the setting for those last dramas in the life of the charismatic Nazarene. In her dream our writer senses that she *is* Stella, who sees through time. And Stella is *seeing*, not dreaming. And still her heart is heavy as she thinks about her daughter.

After staying in Agde for some time, I'd done my reading and thinking. I had dreamed my dreams. In my mind there were now four people who, I knew, would play some important part in my story. I had fragments of truth, fragments of legend and fragments of story in my head. With my psychic character Stella, I was interested in *then* and *there*; like her I was interested in *here* and *now*. And I was interested in the layers in between. I had discovered a story – not explored before - that connected all this into an organic whole. The big task now was to write it.

I finally returned to this house to complete this novel, which I'd planned and thought about for more than two years. I wanted somehow to evoke the timeless and the time-full magic of the place that had first entranced me. But nothing was pre-ordained in the writing. And actually living there, digging deeper and deeper into what I felt about the place, made the original ideas evolve and blossom in ways I could not have foretold.

From *An Englishwoman in France*. Stella wanders through the town:

> That end of the town is more dilapidated than the rue Haute of the Maison d'Estella. I remember what Madame Patrice said. '...the poor gather there, of whom I am one. Bad things are said of them but they are wonderful people.' I pass a rather grand restored house and then I count the wonderful doors, now battered and broken, that were once portals to grand town houses. Some are patched with plywood. Some are daubed in graffiti. On one door is a white handprint on the faded green paint. I wonder now if this has occult meaning. Perhaps it's just a playful gesture.
>
> I try to make my way down a side street but two boys playing football - immaculate in a Nike strip - bar my way. Madame had told me, '...they look after their children, you know. That's a good sign.' The boys stand aside politely, football in hand, as I pass them. Then they smile knowingly when I return, having discovered the dead end. And I have to work hard to push to the back of my mind the thought of those other two footballing boys, locked up now in a cold British prison in a town in the north of England...'

Borrowing Characters from History

A letter from our writer, researching in Agde 2009, to her friend;

Hello my dear,

It's heating up down here. The municipal flower beds are blossoming in an entirely different configuration from those at home. Penstemon, lavender, gaura, marigolds - all subtly planted in an apparently random fashion that mimics the natural wildness of the riverbanks that we saw here earlier this season. A far cry from much brighter, jolly bedding plants packing out the centre of roundabouts at home.

Outside the city, in the vineyards that are everywhere, the plants in their lines are a hot, bright green and the grapes are plumping up under the sheltering leaves. The corn is as high as an elephants knee – it'll be a while before it reaches his eye… And we've actually witnessed the harvesting of a golden field of wheat months before such events back at home.

In the heat, one cool place - in more ways than one - to sit and talk or write is *La Place de la Marine* at the far end of the quayside, past the rather grand cafes bobbing about on their river pontoons. In years gone by this square was where the fishermen would land their catches and they (or their wives) would sell their wares. Lines of ships would have their noses to the quayside, sails furled, ropes wheezing and straining against the big rings in the harbour wall.

But now *la Place de la Marine* is a dappled open space, lined with plane trees which shade blue tables belonging to a small, elegant cafe called *Cafe Capitaine* where charming people bring you coffee, wine, or fine food to fuel your thinking, talking and writing.

Interestingly, inside the cafe is a very colourful, illuminated picture of a large boat. Before it is a small sailing boat where stand our own sailor adventurers, Nira and Allan and their black dog.

Even on the hottest day at this end of the quayside, you can rely on cooling offshore breezes, as well as a chance to catch the last rays of the sun at the end of the day. I've drafted chapters of the new novel here. I've watched children play independently in family groups, the big sisters and brothers taking care of the little ones. I've watched droves of visitors arriving on their bikes, or off the small ferry that works its way up and down the Hérault and stops at this small landing.

The children play around the statue at the centre of the square - a creamy evocation of Aphrodite, spouse of Poseidon, the God of the Sea. She's wielding a paddle and stands atop a globe of the world. This statue is dedicated to navigators who have set out from this place and sailed the world's oceans. Adventurers all.

My own current favourite navigator is a sailor called Jean-Victor Cannac, who made a voyage round the world in 1826 in a ship called l'Astrolobe. The Astrolobe story has royal connections: hoping to find the last traces of an expedition led by a Captain Lapèrouse, which had disappeared in 1788 in the Pacific, King Charles X entrusted the search to a Frigate Captain Jules Dinant d'Urville. This Captain loaded up at Toulon on 7th February 1826 on the corvette L'Astrolobe with a crew of 80 men, one of whom was Jean-Victor Cannac.

Now then! This young man's family owned the *Maison d'Estella* – the house at the centre of my new story! And the Cannac family lived in the house right up to 1916.

We have direct information about nineteen year old Jean-Victor from his sailor's ticket. He stands 1m 60 tall, has black hair which covers his brow; the same colour eyes. He has an oval face, a large nose, a small mouth and a dimpled chin. These fine attributes, his qualities as a sailor, and his willing attitude on board, were much appreciated by the captain who eventually named an unnamed Pacific island after him.

How can any writer resist all this? It is either another novel in itself … oh dear I might have to come back!… or perhaps I might just borrow Jean-Victor as a prime example of brave Agathoise manhood and plant him in the middle of my story - either in the present day or in 300AD .

As everything here, this is all very tempting for a poor writer….

Love, Wendy.

Risk

Picture this: Our writer sits for twenty minutes in her little car outside the long wall of a prison. She wonders why she's here. What made her answer the advertisement, safe in the knowledge her application was late and she would not be considered? Shooting herself in the foot is an old survival strategy. Why is she here? She hates prisons. It's an old joke in her family that she has an aversion to prisons, even refusing to watch fashionable films and documentaries about prisons. She defends herself by saying she thinks that in another life she was imprisoned and anything about prison in this life gives her the heeby-jeebies. The prison people mustn't have noticed that her application was late because here she is, having been invited for an interview.

Eventually she makes her way through the big gates and is handed over to a uniformed apprentice officer who looks about ten years old and takes her on a tour of the prison. He is loud in his talk about prisons and what they mean. He despises the fact that the women here are allowed to wear their own clothes, unlike the men's prison, where he is also apprenticed. There, he says approvingly the men have to wear prison clothing. His contempt for the inmates is obvious.

She lets his voice drone on as, side by side, they walk the gloss-painted, silent corridors. She begins to wonder why this all seems so familiar. Has she dreamt it? Then she realizes that in some way it looks, smells and feels like The Hospital - so embedded in her family tradition - where one Christmas she put up decorations in the Day Room.

This thought makes her breathe out and relax.

In the interview she's careless, says just what she feels, thinking this will make them turn her down. At the end of the interview she asks the governor what will surprise her if she were to come into his prison. 'The laughter,' says the Governor, breaking into a smile 'You'll be surprised by the amount of laughter.'

An hour later the Governor rings her at home and tells her they are happy to offer her the residency. She puts down the phone and stares at it. What on earth has she let herself in for?

Confined

Prison is a hidden place. Myths and mysteries about the nature of prison life live in our minds through literature and film but most of all they reside in the imagination: the dark cupboard under the stairs is with us, whether we have literally experienced it or not. To this nightmare add the notion of *women* in prison. For some outsiders there is a peculiar fascination of women enclosed together, be it medieval nunneries or the gargoyle fiction of women in Cell Block H, the prison soap opera.

Being a Writer in Residence in any prison – as I was for successive periods of three years and two years - is to walk and work on the margins of society. Once in there as writers we only achieve something creative if we empathise with the prisoners in an environment where empathising with prisoners can be seen as perverse and dysfunctional.

Writers experience - as do permanent staff - the borderland between freedom and incarceration. The fact that we go back through the gates at the end of the day does not obviate the fact that for six or more hours we have not been free to act intuitively; to speak off the top of our heads; to hug a person who has made us laugh; to swap gossip about our history, our homes, our lovers and our children.

In this environment we writers have to create a desert island of personal freedom and invite the people we meet – staff as well as prisoners – to join us there. The treasures on my island include great books to read and the opportunity to write out of one's boots, to write hot, and write well. Some things are simple: all you need is a pen and a notebook which you can take back to your 'pad'. As a matter of fact when I first went in notebooks were taboo, so we had to work around that. Things changed, though.

I was helped by my conviction that - inside or outside prison - everyone can learn how to write well, and will certainly write better if they write a lot, with a waiting audience and a willing collaborator in mind. What is different inside is the strong life experience these writers have had, which out-fiction any fiction I have read. This can be exciting but I knew it was important to be aware of the natural tendency in writing your stuff down, to disclose something a person might not have said out loud. Once something has been revealed in writing what do you do with it? I had the blessing of the Governor with the sense of humour, and the good luck in prison to work closely with a professional Avril Joy – later my good friend, and a talented writer herself - who was able to support me in all my strange proposals. My further experience in confinement taught me that, in that strange, surreal, occasionally paranoid world, such people are not always around.

In my residencies, there emerged hundreds of pieces of writing from a wide range of women, a selection of which survive in dozens of pamphlets and leaflets culminating in two books *Why Am I Running*? And *The Self Revealed*. These collections of writing are permanent records of what can seem an ephemeral, sometimes unaccountable experience. Paradoxically this very free activity ticks many boxes in a box-ticking society – the sacred cows on communication, collaboration, intellectual autonomy for a start.

I have to say I was very much a learner within that strong experience. From their disturbing, humourous, illuminating writing I learned about being locked up twenty two hours a day; about the shock of life in the cell and on the wing; about the laughs, the comradeship and the fears; about the lives where breaking the law was the norm; about the mourning for children and loved ones and a former - brighter or more threatening - life outside; about the guilty actions and betrayals, public and private, that led these women through the gates into confinement.

*From **Why Am I Running?** This writer was nineteen years old and had been in some kind of 'care' since she was 11. She wrote poems for other women in exchange for cigarettes and Crunchie bars:*

Why Am I Running?
I'm running quick along the way
Where I'm going I do not know

I'm running faster, my heart is beating
I can't see but I hear my feet

I feel the wind against my face
Why am I running, where am I going?
My heart is pounding in my chest
I see it. I see the figure.

It's so big but it has no face
Is it chasing me? Why am I running?
The browning leaves swiftly fall
Into the night. Rubbish blows along

The days go in. The nights come out
I'm running faster, my heart starts racing
The stars are there, shining so bright
I wish I was on the moon.

In our confinement - as well as the books, we wrote a radio play; one young Chinese woman, now safely back in China, wrote a clever short story that was broadcast by the BBC; one woman used her writing collection to illustrate her state of mind which helped to secure more appropriate sentencing. We participated in the international *Changing Lives Through Literature Project* mounting *a* version of Professor Robert Waxler's Changing Lives Through Literature project. We also visited him in Boston Massachusetts to observe his great project in action. We invented the first *Litfest Inside*, where the women worked with seven published writers in fourteen days. We had two performances of women's work for insiders and outsiders. We initiated a shadow *Orange Project* where women, read, discussed and reviewed the shortlisted books for the Orange Prize.

One only has to work inside prison to realise that the logistics of doing any or all these things, under the constraints of prison rules and culture, is almost impossible. Almost. But what *was* possible, what *was* the most wonderful thing, was that for a few hours a day we writers from the outside and the inside could inhabit our Desert Island and remind ourselves of our unique humanity and remember we were citizens of the world.

Working in such a residency is the opposite of the cloistered, isolated, working life of a writer. But it was inspiring and life-changing for me, fostering insights I could never have imagined, never arrived at through academic research. This sharing of other people's experience of confinement has indirectly but inevitably crept into my own writing. Amongst other novels that have been certainly affected by these insights into confinement, I wrote about it directly when reflecting on the lives of women in internment camps in Singapore, in my novel *The Long Journey Home,* which I will come to in the next chapter. As well as this I've written many short stories in an attempt to get to grips with the strength of that unique experience. Five of these have found a place in the Knives collection.

*From the short story **Chaos** in the **Knives** Collection (2009):*

> ...So lets get back to this screaming of brakes. This noise of traffic in my ear. The lions roaring like people. The people growling like lions. And this girl! Her hand was digging in my shoulder. I could hardly see her through the haze, but she I knew from the very scent of her she was young. What was she saying? ...

*And from **The Woman Who Drew Buildings** (2008):*

> ... But prison had succeeded where Sam with all his cocky charm had failed. Inside prison, smoking tobacco was the least-worst thing you could do to numb the pain, to while away the time...Of course prison had been a shock, terrifying. But in the end it was not as hard as Adam first feared. The worst thing was being warehoused and moved around like an object, with no sovereignty over

your body, your possessions, or your daily routines. The fear inside those places was not about what *happened* but about what *might* happen: that something bad *might* happen even when in the end it didn't. Dark tales and myths about what had happened to others in this same place flew about the place like black moths. Being suspended in such uncertainty could twang the steadiest of nerves and in the end he learned that a smoke could steady the nerves…

At The Hotel Keong Sak

From **The Long Journey Home** *(2002):*

The Cathay Cinema, tucked into the bottom of Singapore's highest building, was packed with customers keen to enjoy the dark charms of Vivien Liegh in *Gone With The Wind*. Two thirds of the customers were in uniform, among them members of the Singapore Volunteers, the British Army, the Australian Army, the Indian Army and the Royal Navy. RAF uniforms were thin on the ground. Soldiers and citizens muttered in the streets about this matter. The more informed gossips knew that the lack of air cover was also a bone of contention between the civilian and military high-ups in Singapore and their masters in London. Those in London had other things on their minds. For them the war in the Middle East was much more important than this alleged threat from the Japanese. Even so, they continued to protest, weren't they pouring into the city from all over The Empire? This was undeniable. But still they were criminally short of aircraft.

Singapore would have to wait its turn.

Picture this: Our writer now has a teaching career behind her and feels able to write *writer* on her passport, although she doesn't quite believe it. Even so she's written a good number of novels, many of them inaccurately labelled *saga*. One of these, just completed, would be more accurately labelled an *historical novel*.

It begins with the fall of Singapore to the Japanese in February 1942.

Her research for this novel has been thorough. She has read a hundred books and built a time line. She has pored over cotemporaneous maps of the island. She has looked at the esoteric sites on the internet. She has sourced and read a hundred letters to his wife from the Master of the Singapore Shipyards, one of whose responsibilities was to marshall the fleets of warships anchored there – the great insurance, according to the London government, against any Japanese attack. She has even read the wartime biography of General Tomoyuki Yamashita, the Japanese commander (in translation, of course…). Yamashita recounts his strategy of invading Singapore by coming down the Malaysian peninsula and attacking the island of Singapore via the causeway - a strategy that ensured what was seen as a shameful defeat in the annals of British warfare.

But – most importantly, as she sees herself as an historian of private lives - our writer has wept in the round tower of the Imperial War Museum as she read the diaries and fragments of letters of the individual women who were interned on Singapore by the Japanese occupiers.

Her novel about this defeat and these women had been inspired some years before by a tale from her neighbour, Bob, who as a young officer had participated in the relief of Singapore in 1945. One of his tasks was at the Raffles Hotel, allotting accommodations to some of the women emerging from the internment camps, before they embarked for home.

A story keeps cropping up in in our writer's research, about children who were somehow lost or left behind in the rush to quayside, to get on the boats and flee. She reads one story about a boy – picked up in the early fifties - who had been taken by a Malay family and brought up as Malay, speaking no English,

Our girl thinks she's a good researcher. And she thinks now she can put this novel together. She believes she has got the history, the climate, the elusive feeling of being alive at that time. She wakes up one morning with a girl named Sylvie on her mind: Sylvie is eight years old, the age she herself had been when she lost her own Daddy. What if Sylvie had been left behind in the rush for the boats? Who would help her? Now, into Sylvie's story walks Virginia Chen, Sylvie's teacher, left behind quite deliberately because she's not European…

From **The Long Journey Home** *(2002)* Bo Sambuck, having seen (so he thinks) his family, including his daughter Sylvie - onto a boat, returns to his role in the Singapore Volunteers to defend his city. In another part of the city Virginia Chen writes her journal. Bo reflects on the situation:

> … The talk in the crowd had been that the Japanese had come down the peninsula and were on their way, pushing the Australians and Indians aside like flies. How changed things were. Wasn't the city full of soldiers, some drunk, who were even competing with the woman and children to get away? Bo wondered why they weren't rushing in the opposite direction, to the front line, to stop Yamashita's onrush.
>
> There must be some strategy behind it: some last-ditch saving of the city. But he couldn't for the life of him think what it was.

Virginia Chen: Her Book

> I must confess to a feeling of anger as Ah So and I stood with our back to the dusty wall and let the crowd surge past us, carrying my Sylvie and the Sambucks with it. Part of my anger was seeing these people – once compact, phlegmatic, self-contained Europeans – pressing forward like a flock of fleeing pigeons. Some moved in a solid way, trudging forward in a dazed fashion; some cried and panicked, pushed and screamed. We were even treated to the sight of uniformed soldiers using their rifles to press their way through: these soldiers who had come to defend our city,
>
> I reflect that these fluttering, fleeing pigeons were the people we had been taught to respect; to acknowledge their greater right to the overlord-ship of our land.

It was in the newspaper. The Governor said he would take care of all the people on the island. None of those at risk would be left to the mercy of the Japanese. Then there was another announcement, from the British Government Envoy, to say that there would only be places for Europeans: that we were indeed to be left.

I am most angry with myself for believing these myths of respect that they have fed us. It occurs to me that I have been on the wrong side in my arguments with my brother Simon.

And what of Miss Sylvie Sambuck, my protégée, my own little pigeon? I wonder how she will fare under the tender mercy of Mrs Sambuck? She's in for some beatings, that's for sure...

By the time I travelled to Singapore with my friend Avril Joy, Sylvie and Virginia Chen had - among other things - experienced together the invasion, the internment and the liberation of Singapore and the novel was now finished: in its very final draft. Now I only had a few things to think about, to feel, to sort out in my own mind while I was actually on the island.

Avril and I stayed at the *Hotel Keong Sak*, a cheap, clean hotel near the old Chinese quarter. We discovered from an amused taxi driver that the Keong Sak Street happened to be a famous street for brothels. We laughed at this. The joy of travelling with Avril is that there is always laughter.

My job on this stay was to uncover 1942 Singapore beneath the affluent high rise glamour of 21st Century Singapore. And after my years of poring over maps and absorbing personal histories I really felt I was able to do that. The hotel was very noisy because of the cheap air-conditioning unit attached to its outside walls. The air was filled with the smell of spicy food from the nearby street food kiosks. Going out of the hotel was like walking into an oven. Of course, here in 1940, not even cheap, noisy air-conditioning was available for the European women. Some of them – second and third generation residents

- would be acclimatised. But some of the women had only just arrived on the island, urged on by their husbands, to come to the 'safety' of Singapore, out of Blitz-ridden England.

As the days passed I became aware of the power of the teatime downpour – a benevolent refreshment, very unlike rainfall in Britain. I felt that this rain would have been so appreciated in the internment camp. In this season it must have been a welcome chance to get clean, rinse their hair, wash what clothes they had left. One day, leaning out of the window of the *Keong Sak,* we watched a building labourer – very dark skinned with a film-star glamour – stand with his face up to the warm drenching rain, rubbing his hands, face, arms and legs with soap, as though he were in a shower. Again I thought of the women doing this, of course without the soap.

All the time I was there on the island, these women were in my heart and my mind: swept up from the dock, mopped up from the shores of islands when their boats had been shot from under them, leaving behind their pretty houses, their secure jobs, herded into the camps where they would live – if they survived - in fear and squalor, in too close quarters - for three and a half years. At the liberation some of them were welcomed at Raffles by my friend Bob before they took their *Long Journey Home.* He is in my story, this young officer from County Durham.

In the novel, after the war, Sylvie eventually makes her way back home with Virginia. Her mother – who got away without her – does not treat her kindly and they are very estranged. I wrote about this encounter intuitively; it worked well within the logic of the story I'd invented. Six months after the novel came out I had a letter from a woman in the South of England asking *how did you know? Did it happen to you?* She went on to say that she too had been left behind in the rush from Singapore. When she finally got back home after the liberation her mother was very cold and rejecting, which made her very unhappy. Consequently she was in therapy for many years, and really never recovered from this experiences. But, she said, when she read this novel she cried again and again over two or three days. It had been the first time she'd cried since she got home from Singapore more than fifty years before.

'*It was wonderful,*' she wrote. '*Thank you so much for that.*'

Early on in our stay in Singapore Avril came across a young man in an internet café called Peter Lee, an accountant. Peter kindly offered to drive us around for small fee. I'd located the camp on one of my maps so I asked him to take us there. He was puzzled at the location, which was on the edge of a rather glamorous golf course. But when we got there his smooth brow became smoother. 'Ah!' he said, grinning. 'I know it! This was a shooting range. We practised shooting here when I did my military training.' He told us all the young men on Singapore did compulsory military service. Their war games had to be carried out in other countries, though, because Singapore island was much too small.

Of course, from my busy-bee researching I knew all there was to know about Singapore history but Peter - while polite – was not interested. He knew less than me. He was a modern man in a modern world. He looked forward, not back. Good thing too.

However his answer to one of my questions was crucial. In the novel Sylvie flies kites with Virginia Chen's brother. I had them flying their kites in the Botanic Gardens. When I got there I realised that this would have been impossible because of the high tree-canopy: almost no breeze.

'So where would you fly a kite on Singapore?' I asked.

He grinned broadly. 'Ah! I will show you a place where they have flown kites for hundreds of years.'

He drove us, then, to a beach, lapped by the sparkling South China Sea, not far from the glittering high rise business buildings that now dominate the Singapore skyline and define it as a modern city. So that's where, in the novel, Sylvie flies her kite.

One night, coming back from a restaurant to the *Keong Sak* Avril and I jumped the taxi queue and accepted the offer of a ride on a rickshaw pulled by an old wiry man. We were doubtful about our combined weight at first but he beamed and shook his head. 'I very strong!' he said, flexing his arm muscles. 'I very strong!' He held the rickshaw in balance while we climbed aboard and then we were away, holding on for dear life, careering in the direction of the *Keong Sak*. On the way we circled an enormous four-lane roundabout, running parallel to, and being overtaken by, sleek limousines and smart cars. Back at the *Keong Sak,* we laughed till we cried.

From **Long Journey Home**. Young Sylvie Sambuck has been lost in the rush for the boats and is still in the city under attack:

Sylvie sat on the veranda and looked back over the town. She could see dense smoke rising from the godowns and she could smell the burning rubber. Down there in Chinatown there were flames shooting up like candles. And above it all was the quickly darkening blue sky skewered by two red streaks of sunset. Again the tears started. She wiped them away with a dirty hand. She stood up. Very soon the sky would be pitch-dark.

The house – her own home for all of her life – now seemed threatening and strange. It was no place for her. No place at all.

She padded down the gravel drive and climbed over the gate. She wouldn't have been surprised if the rickshaw man had gone off with all her bags and boxes. But no, he was there, smoking a skinny cigarette. He balanced the rickshaw and she clambered aboard.

'Now Beach Road,' she said.

'Many houses blow down, Missee,' he said.

'Not all of them. My friend Miss Chen lives in number nineteen. Long time after the Raffles Hotel. That not blow down.'

She felt the load move and the rickshaw settle to a heavy rhythm in time with his plodding steps. She looked at his narrow corded back topped by the wide cone of his hat and closed her eyes trying to remember what he looked like from the front. She could only remember the broken toothed smile. She couldn't remember whether he had a young strong face, like Simon Chen's, or an old wrinkled face like Miss Chen's grandma...

The Story Teller's Apprentice (1)

The boy and girl on the beach are now both very grown up, but like their mother, they still have words in their hearts and stories up their sleeves. The little girl who spent hours contemplating crabs and sea creatures is *very* grown up now - a professional journalist, an editor and a fine writer about food and every other kind of thing. She also continues to be a great inspiration, an important part of the conspiracy of ideas from which my stories emerge. She is always mounting surprises. My novel *The Self Made Woman,* set in Moscow in 1991, is entirely down to her inspiration.

Picture this: Our writer is visiting her daughter who is living in Moscow. She has missed her daughter, who has been in Russia for nearly a year. She is excited by the opportunity. From her academic studies she knows the history right from Catherine the Great through Peter the Great to Lenin, Trotsky and Stalin. She is familiar with the legend of the Gulags, to the economic imperative of Centralised Planning and the Primitive Accumulation of Capital which - at great price - dragged this country into the status of superpower which made it the bogeyman of the Cold War.

Just before her 1991 visit she'd seen the headlines.

TANKS ON RED SQUARE

Coup attempt. Yeltsin stands on a tank to defy the August Coup

As a child of the Cold War our writer is nervous about the visit - having incorporated the sensational accounts of Soviet post war pulchritude into her subconscious. Our writer's mother Barbara had a bit of a soft spot for the Russians, for pulling the Nazis off our backs during the war. She also used to mention with, dark delight, Russians marching in *with snow on their boots*.

Our writer knows that this will be a momentous visit for her so she keeps assiduous notebooks, making lists, drawing what she sees, scribbling into the night in the small, elegant flat in the Foreigners Block. Her daughter's boyfriend mutters darkly about 'your mother scribbling away, all about us…' But he's not nearly as interesting as this strange city, up close now after a lifetime of wondering.

One day they are walking the dilapidated streets of Moscow when her daughter stops just before a corner and makes her mother close her eyes. Once around the corner she is allowed to open them and before her is a small, exquisite church newly painted in pale bright blue, topped by a newly gilded onion dome. Her breath catches in her throat. She knows she is seeing history, seeing Russia reclaiming its past.

Later at a diplomatic party at the American embassy, our writer sees a neat older woman with well cut hair on the other side of the room, in a smart, slightly old fashioned suit. 'She's interesting,' her daughter whispers in her ear. 'her daughter's a famous American journalist on assignment here. The mother came to visit three years ago, fell in love with Moscow, went back to America, gave up her job, sold her house and car and came back here.'

This woman – in her sixties - had come back to live as Russian (not in the privileged journalist/diplomatic circles, but as Russian – a difficult thing in those days). She worked for a living as a doctor's assistant and seemed to be thriving.

All this is like a great bell resounding through our writer. What if it were an Englishwoman who did this extraordinary thing? What if she were a children's writer looking for a new life and new inspiration? What if the daughter is a bit of an egotist…?

Later, back home from her exciting visit, our writer picks up the newspaper and sees an article about a very old woman who has been found in Russia and has been there since before the Revolution when – like many indigent English girls – she had been employed as a nanny by an aristocratic family.

Put it all together, our writer thinks, *and there is a great story.*

Five years later, with the help of her many Russian notebooks, her bulging file and a collage of images on her study wall, she writes the novel.

From *The Self Made Woman* (1999) Caitlin, a journalist, has come upon her mother Olivia with a strange Russian man, making love in her Moscow flat. There is an old woman dozing in a chair. Olivia is wearing her daughter's negligèe. She narrates:

'The old woman is his *aunt*?'

I shake my head slowly, uncertain of the wisdom of the next revelation. 'No. She's not. It seems she's actually English.'

'What?' Caitlin's face becomes keen, loses its tiredness.

'I don't know the whole story yet. She was employed by a Russian family in England before the First World War and came here with them, just a very young girl. Somehow she must have been stuck here, become Russian. She's been talking to me. Her English was very rusty at first but when she got started she managed very well. Old fashioned English, northern accent. It was like sitting with your ear to a time machine, Caitlin. She got very tired though. We had to let her sleep.'

I can feel Volodya's amusement.

'You *talked* to her?' Caitlin's whole demeanour has changed. Her aggression has seeped from her like water into sand. Her face is now bright and sharp. Once I saw a police dog being given the clothes of a missing child and it started straining at the leash. Caitlin has just such a look. 'Good heavens, mother! What a story!'

She is already on the phone...

London Calling

My friends know I hate to be referred to as a *regional* writer or a *local* writer. I don't identify with the localised cosiness of these terms nor the patronising pigeon-holing involved - convenient to journalists, commentators and the marketing departments of publishers. And this pigeon-holing is more so for what some people see as a certain *kind* of writer. There is no such label for writers who cling to London or other parts of Britain for their inspiration. We don't label Martin Amis, Ian McEwan, Nick Hornby, Thomas Hardy, D H Lawrence, Ian Rankin or Val McDermid as regional writers. The descriptor *regional* seems to me to be a keeping-down kind of word, know-your-place kind of word, a clogs-and-shawls kind of word, a story-but-no-intellect kind of word, a chip-on-the-shoulder kind of word. I reject it.

The Americans, not as hidebound by the peculiarities of literary snobbery as we are, are much better at this. After all, many of their greatest and most respected writers are from vastly different regions. Some of them write wonderfully and to great acclaim about localised domestic life and the intricacy of family deception, secrets, loss, and the need for identity.

Don't get me wrong, I love my area of England and identify with its beauty and its complexities with a passion, even though I only came here when I was eight, when my father died. And, after I filtered out my mother's dislike for the North, I have always rejoiced in the region. But the notion that my region is *all* that I am and *all* that I can be is reductive and careless.

My grandparents and great grandparents came from all parts of the British Isles so I don't 'belong' to any region. I see myself as belonging to the human race, that's all. You will see from this book that my inspiration springs out of this place but travels to many different places both in the interior world of individuals and out there in the real world.

Regional presses are naturally very loyal to their writers which I think is wonderful. I do understand why they look for the local angle in all of their stories. But I'm afraid the marketing departments of publishers jump on this easy *regional* bandwagon and lack the imaginative energy to think beyond that.

However for writers to succeed, their appeal has to reach quite beyond their county boundaries. So you can see why I rejoice in the letters that come to me from all parts of Britain and delight in my PLR returns, which tells me my novels are borrowed nearly two hundred thousand times a year from libraries across Britain. And that, through the library system, they reach appreciative readers in Canada, New Zealand and Australia.

I often feel like reminding people that *Britain* is my region and *London* - which I knew intimately through my wide reading before I ever set foot in it – is my City. It's not far away: just a couple of hours from here on the train. I've been going up and down to London for more than twenty years, researching my books, seeing my publishers and my agents.

From the beginning I always liked getting away from the North and down to London: I liked being alone there, in a small hotel by the British Museum. I loved sitting in the beautiful round Reading Room in Bloomsbury, working on my novels, in a space where Karl Marx wove his world vision, Oscar Wilde wove his aphorisms, Bram Stoker wove his nightmares, and George Orwell imagined his dark futures. Virginia Woolf had worked there, as had Mahatma Gandhi, Muhammad Ali Jinnah, Rudyard Kipling, George Bernard Shaw, Mark Twain, Lenin, Arthur Rimbaud and H. G. Wells. This place reflected much of the flesh and blood of my reading.

I once met my first agent there for lunch and we looked at the Jane Austen manuscripts. It was comforting to see the scribbles and amendments of this impeccable writer. The joy of putting just the right word in the right place is visible in her drafts. I identified with her completely and love the fact that she is the mistress of writing about localised domestic life and the intricacy of family deception, secrets, loss, and the need for security and identity. This was before, of course, the labelling of such writers as *regional* writers.

One day I was in the Reading Room, researching bare-knuckle fighting for what was to be my novel *Kitty Rainbow*. In a folder of loose documents I discovered my Ishmael, the man who found and named the eponymous Kitty. He plays a big role in the novel.

From **Kitty Rainbow** *(1988):*

...By the time the tall woman got right up to the ringside the drumming had stopped, the young man had vanished, and a boxing match was underway. A short square man announced the fight between Ishmael Slaughter and Gypsy Joe Elliot. Her ears pounded as the crowd roared and the dogs barked. Then, interested despite herself, the woman watched as the two big men squared up to each other.

The fighter called Ishmael was in his middle years, a magnificent figure of a man with a large open face and a broken nose; his mane of black and silver hair was held back by a leather thong. Gypsy Joe was a much younger man with a massive muscular physique. He had the colouring and flashing good looks of his clan, not unlike those of the woman selling heather at the edge of the crowd.

Both men moved surprisingly lightly for their great size, ducking and dodging, diving and swerving so that for several minutes no hit found its spot, The crowd was yelling in disappointment, denied its first blood, There was no taste for the new 'scientific' boxing in this crowd.

The woman was reminded of the baying of wolves that she'd heard once, somewhere on the Eastern borders of Germany.

'Go to it, Ishmael! Cut the bugger down!' yelled the short man who had parted the crowd for her.

It was in the British Museum Reading Room that, by accident, I found papers regarding a murder in North Yorkshire, where a woman farm worker had killed her employer. The papers included an intriguing verbatim account of the trial, including a list of the jurors which included *T Wetherill, Auctioneer.* This man's son was my Grandfather Tom Wetherill, who lost a fortune and ended up as chief male attendant at The Hospital, so important in my own story here.

Perhaps one day, I will turn this story of the murder of the farmer, his maidservant and the jury man into a novel. It would be exciting to write about a character based on my great grandfather, whom I never knew...

I have always enjoyed being the stranger in London, sitting in cafes watching the cosmopolitan mixture of people - so different from my virtually mono-cultural North. I remember pacing round and round Bedford Square one day. to make sure that I arrived just on time for my first meeting with my editor at Hodder and Stoughton, the lovely Linda Jennings, to talk about *Lizza,* my first long young adult book. I was wearing a brown velvet A-line dress with a white ruffle collar. As a good working class girl, dressing one's best is *de rigeur* - good manners for special occasions. In fact I was rather over-dressed. Everyone in the office was dressed in demure, even dusty, black and white - my first big lesson in Town and Country values.

And I remember some years later, pacing up and down Oxford Street, waiting for the time to be right to meet for the first time the excellent Anne Williams at Headline Publishers, who have since published most of my adult novels. We were to discuss *Riches of The Earth*, my first adult novel. Anne wore a large black felt hat with a big swept-back brim. It was such a relief when she took it off in the restaurant and put it on the seat beside her, to reveal a neat girl with a pale, sharp, clever face. I learned such a great deal from Anne about the architecture of big novels and the subtleties of style and pacing. She was a great editor.

My new agent, Juliet Burton sold *Riches of The Earth* to Headline at her first offer. I'd never heard of this company but was so engaged by Juliet's certainty that, though this was the second year of its existence, Headline was the publisher of the future. Three years later Headline won the prestigious Publisher of the Year Award, so Juliet was right. In the years since Juliet's prophecy the company has gone from strength to strength. I have been with Headline for more than twenty years and have had several editors since Anne Williams - two of whom have since become full time novelists themselves: gamekeepers turned poachers perhaps...

Juliet was my second agent. I sold *Lizza* myself, with no mentors, no friends at court, just by picking a publisher out of the Writers' and Artists' Yearbook. I sent the manuscript to Andre Deutsch and Hodder and Stoughton. Linda Jennings at Hodder accepted it right away. That was a *very* happy day.

When I met Linda and babbled out my writing plans she said I definitely needed an agent to field all these ideas. She recommended someone, a person who had been at one of the big agencies and was making her way. It seemed very suitable, and this woman turned out to be very nice – sharp and savvy with lots of anecdotes about publishing. On reflection we rarely talked constructively about my writing or my way forward in publishing but I found out a lot about her and the stresses in her life.

I think it was my misfortune to meet this woman when she was on the edge of some kind of breakdown. She was certainly in no condition to help me develop my career or sell my books. Linda Jennings took the next two young adult books for Hodder and Stoughton without the agent having to do anything. There was a hiccup about the next book (a pretty good novel, actually about children and a dog-track...) and she was no use to me at all. Things started to go wrong. The paperwork went astray and I was not certain about the handling of the money. I don't really know what happened, but - as happens with depressed people - she ducked below the radar and I was forced to sever my connection with her. Decades later I recovered royalties which had been lying dormant on the French edition of one of the books in this agent's care.

I retired hurt myself, for a while. This was the time, referred to earlier, when I really *did* look into the abyss. Then I started to write what I saw as my first 'big' adult novel, stumbling a little as I went. Then, encouraged - as I said above in *Only Connect* - by John McGahern, I finished the novel. Now, I thought, I really needed a new agent. Resorting again to the Writers' and Artists' Year Book, I found Juliet Burton, then senior agent at Laurence Pollinger. She was pleased to offer the novel and - as I've said here - sold it to Headline at first go. She later went solo and I was happy to go with her, pushing out of my mind my earlier bad experience with another agent who also 'went solo'.

Juliet has been my mentor ever since, offering me useful advice, calming me when I panic, being a sounding board for my new wild ideas - including this book. She is a very shrewd first reader without (as many agents like to nowadays) taking on the bustling mantle of editor. Everyone works differently but I try never to present less that what I feel is a finished manuscript and don't expect Juliet to work on drafts. Still, her shrewd and helpful suggestions always have an impact on the novel in hand. She is a very good egg in publishing terms and now a good friend.

So as a writer I was obliged to embrace London as one of my inspirations because publishing in Britain is dominated by London and to be alive to London, on its streets, in its buses in its cafes and libraries, has been a source of pleasure in my writing life.

And now in more recent years I've had the special delight of my own base in London as my daughter - she who liked crabs and sea creatures and showed me the magic of Moscow - now lives in London. I knew it was only a matter of time before I wrote a novel based in London. I realised that now, London could be incorporated into my *region* and all would be well. One novel *My Dark Eyed Girl* – about a girl fighter in the Spanish Civil War – has a very located London sequence, but *The Lavender House* is set entirely in London.

From ***The Lavender House*** *(2007)* Here are Sophia's (possibly mistaken) first impressions of London:

> ....I acquired this habit of looking obliquely at people
> when I first came to London. Here, direct looks cause
> embarrassment, seem like an invasion, a challenge. It's

seen as disrespectful and can generate violence, even death. It's on the news every night: a shooting here, a stabbing there, a mugging in another place. All dark and violent but everyday stuff here.

Up in Newcastle we tell ourselves we live in a safe place. Warm. Authentic. Even there you can feel threatened, but it is more diluted, less 'everyday'. The press of people is less. It's still very dangerous though, if you're in the wrong place or in the wrong family. I found this to my cost.

Here in London this low level feeling of threat can diminish you. But at its best it's a buzz, a challenge, London. It keeps you on your toes. Every look is an exchange to be dealt with. The default reaction is avoidance and so many of these subtle avoidances can lead to weariness, dark exhaustion. When I first came here I used to fall into bed with exhaustion at ridiculously early hours. Of course in those early days I was still recovering from my own dark insanity, that terrible happening in Newcastle, so nothing was what you could call normal. You couldn't really blame London for that.

But I have escaped from that insanity and now in my newly sane world I want to write for a living. So as part of the course I'm obliged to deliver my story by four o'clock in the afternoon. To do this I have to break that avoidance barrier time and time again.

To be honest this has really been like a forcing ground for rudeness. When I mentioned this theory to another student he drawled something about me being a thin-skinned Northerner so I've learned to shut up. Journalism, in legend and often in reality, sees itself as a hard-boiled profession. Clichés abound. *'If it bleeds, it* leads.' 'Don't let the truth get in the way of a good story.' 'Door-stepping is legitimate news gathering.'

The bus swayed and I flinched as something – a knitting needle – poked me in the side.

My course assignment was to take the No 73 bus and find my story: a colour feature about life in the city. I now know the No 73. Catch it in one direction you're heading for the British Museum, Bloomsbury, the West End. Today I have caught it in the opposite direction....

Story Teller's Apprentice (2)

Picture this: This morning, after yesterday, which had been filled by a long publisher's lunch, where her editor tucked in and she ate very little, our writer has been for breakfast with her daughter in a Turkish Café on Stoke Newington High Street. It is next to the police station and the two of them compete in spotting who are the officers in *mufti*. Her daughter suggests they go home through the streets a different way and, as always, the writer follows her daughter's lead. On one corner her daughter links her arm. 'Close your eyes!' she says. Just like Moscow. Our writer wonders if there'll be another blue church with the cupola covered in gold leaf.

But no. Here is a narrow house, with a narrow front garden, dwarfed by its taller, rackety neighbours: even at a glance she reckons it's much older than they are. Beside the narrow front door is an overflowing wheelie bin. She blinks. The house is painted an unlikely shade of pale lavender.

'It has *something,*' she says. All sorts of feelings engulf her. She thinks about her Auntie Lily, who was psychic.

Her daughter pulls her away, towards her own tall, rackety, elegant house on this gentrifying street. 'You think so?' she says.

Later, over a very good glass of red wine – her daughter knows about wine as well as food – she hears the story of the Lavender House. A friend of her daughter lives there with her baby son. She has been haunted by callers, asking her about the house. One of them finally tells her it was associated in the 1960s with the Krays. Just around the corner from this house is the house where in the 60s the gangster Reggie Kray killed Jack McVitie, proving to his psychotic brother Ronnie that he was equally *hard*.

The girl's unwelcome visitor also tells her there is a cellar. Doesn't she know there's a cellar? She shakes her head. There is no cellar. She shoos him away. Later – perhaps a day or weeks later - she lifts the carpet and there indeed is the ring pull for a cellar door. She lifts it up and there is the cellar hole. On the wooden collar to the cellar hole are deep scratch marks.

Listening to the dark sting in the tail of her daughter's story, our writer lets out a breath and puts down her glass, absorbing the terrible image, She takes another very deep breath, knowing there is a great story here. But nobly she tells her daughter that *she* should write the story. Equally nobly she waits nearly four years before she writes her own story about *The Lavender House*.

From ***The Lavender House*** *(2007)* Sophia is finally living in The Lavender House, having fallen off the No 73 bus, had other adventures, and fallen in love with this narrow house in the gentrifying street:

> ....I scrubbed my face hard and sat brushing my hair too long, trying to reassure myself that I was not becoming obsessed with Bobbi Marsh. She was in a strange set-up but she was not neglected. She didn't need my protection. She wouldn't fall through the cracks like Drina had in Newcastle. In any case I was not really responsible for her, like I'd been for Drina. Was I?
>
> Then tears started to fall down my cheeks. Even now they occasionally did this thing. In my job in social work I'd learned to be rational and stoical, even if I wasn't as hard and pragmatic as some of my colleagues. But since those events around Drina I'd cried a Lake Windermere for her, for me, for all the lost children. At first I cried all the time. Then the doctor gave me the pills. When I was taking them I didn't cry all the time. I just cried regularly at certain triggers - a mother chastising her child in a supermarket; a mother skipping with her child in a playground; a Benetton advert for children's clothes. The television was the worst; a child crying in a street in Iraq;

an NSPCC appeal with a child crouching in a corner; a sentimental presentation of some tragic child in a soap opera. In the end I just stopped watching television. Couldn't afford the paper hankies, could I?

But I hadn't cried at all in London. Not till today. Now I sniffed hard and blinked and the tears stopped. When I set out to catch the bus twenty minutes later, there was a man standing in the road looking at the Lavender House. He was wearing mousey clothes. He had a mousey face.

I tucked away my key and went down my path.

'You live here, darlin'?' he said.

'Yes.'

'Is it for sale?'

Another one! 'No. I live here. It's not for sale.'

He put his hand on the gate and I shuddered, as though his hand was on me. 'D'you rent it?' His face was whiter, harder.

'No business of yours.'

'You do, then. So it could be for sale?'

'No. Like I say. I live here. I have a contract.'

'Can I just have a look round it?'

The man must have thought I was a fool. 'You most certainly can't.'

He grinned suddenly, showing over-white teeth. 'Don't get your shirt off, darlin'.' His face had taken on that mild-mouse look again. 'I'll be on my way then.' But he still stared at me.

'You'd better be on your way.' I said. 'Of course I could get the police here.' I turned back and let myself in the house, locked the door behind me and raced upstairs to watch him through the curtains. The man was walking away slowly. Once he turned round and stood in the road, his hands on his hips, staring at the house and up at me in the window. He looked so much like a pantomime villain that I laughed and shook my head. He turned and walked away round the corner, quickly now.

My gaze was pulled to the other end of the street where Julia was decanting her garden spade and fork from her basket. I thought perhaps I would call at Mr Shaheen's on my way back from the lecture. Bobbi could help me paint the yard. That would keep both our minds off this bizarre situation.

Onto The Page

Notebooks

From **Family Ties** *(2005)* Rosa (63) a children's writer reflects:

> … And on. Sitting here with my soft fountain pen, reminding myself of my own pain laid out there in the Tick Book, I suddenly realise that in writing that book I learned to write consistently for the first time, a habit that has stayed with me all these years. (Without it would I have become a writer?) I supposed modern counselling gurus would say that when I wrote in the Tick Book I had *managed to externalise, to heel the scars and somehow learned to heal myself.* (I can hear those words in a faintly transatlantic accent.) How little do they know! In all probability fixing that time in words is the reason why time and again I cling to the enclosed world of childhood in my stories, which are read now by so many children. Not entirely healed, then… It merely demonstrates how and why I've spent most of my adult life in a dream world, at one remove from reality. Not a grown-up way to go about things, you might say.

On my shelves beside me as I write are nearly a hundred notebooks – some A5, but mostly A4. Most of them are hard-bound although some – mistakes – are irritatingly ring-bound. Here are millions of words that I've written by hand before transcribing them onto the computer.

All writers have their own methods of working and there is no magic method. In fact all writers have their own individualised magic methods. Mine is first to draft my work into notebooks. I even have my own statistic - three large bound A4 notebooks expand into one hundred thousand word novel.

I can see that the computer works for many writers who have used them from childhood and find them free and loose enough to allow the liberal intermixing of the powers of the subconscious, the imagination and the intellect which is necessary for writing a novel. I need to write by hand to do this. I need to write by hand with – like Rosa – a soft ink pen in bound lined books. I write only on the right side of the page. This 'only writing on the right hand side' is a present to my child-self because I used to hate writing on the left hand side of the page. However, these days the left hand side of the page is very useful, becoming scrawled with amendments and changes as I edit the hand-written draft.

How does this process work? I don't know. I just know that writing with an ink-pen or a soft pencil is somehow the equivalent of thinking freely, of musing, of speculating. It is scribbling, relaxing into your subconscious, uncovering your dream-trance state. Compared with this, writing straight onto the screen is tense and intense. On the screen your prose is too perfectly presented, too soon. At the computer you have to sit up to attention, use the right fingers, get the syntax right the first time. You are locked into a system that has a tool-bar and a flashing email reminder and too easy a resort to the internet to check facts or situations, to say something witty on Twitter, to see who's looked at your blog, who's just texted you. Sitting at the computer, the World Wide Web crowds in on you. To write well you need to be alone and enjoy being alone. The contemporary fear of being alone, nannied by machines, militates against this.

After I have written ten thousand words or so in my notebook and edited them with scribbles and questions I will transcribe chapters onto my computer. The transcription is another big edit, as I make more changes and amendments to the prose even as it goes onto the screen, trying always to put the right word into the right place, give birth to a more telling metaphor, make the narrative more coherent, more consistent. Once on the computer your prose becomes more fixed in content but more amenable to shaping, adjusting as a whole.

Inconsistencies become more visible, the movement of my characters through time and space begins to require more evident logic.

With pages of print on the screen one inevitably becomes more aware of one's readers, one's audience. This is an approximation of what they will see on the page. Will it work? I ask myself.

Ah, you might say, why not put it straight onto the screen and make it easier for yourself? I tried that once but found it frustrating, rigid and limiting so I returned to my much more labour-intensive, productive free-flowing pen-paper-bound notebook routine. Writing this, I realise that the first highly worked hand-written draft is for *oneself* and ensures that you are being true to yourself as a writer The first drafts must always be just for yourself. Once it gets onto the computer it belongs to the world – your agent, your editor, your publishers, your readers.

But, in its right place – the point of later editing – the computer is a marvellously fluid and flexible instrument and the instant fact-checking is a great boon at these later stages. What used to take me days to check can take me less than a minute using this marvellous machine,

As an aside, I know some writers who draft by hand like me and employ some well-paid secretary to transcribe for them. I think they miss a trick here. So many interesting changes and developments happen at the point of transcription to the computer. The creativity of the hand-written draft infuses the first word-processed draft, setting the tone for the complete novel and the only person who can do that is the writer. The only brain/subconscious/imagination that can make this process work is that of the writer – me, you, any writer.

Visualisation, Collages and Collations

The notebook in which I draft my novel is only *one* kind of notebook, Before that come notebooks filled with observations, lists, notes, inspirations, questions and speculations addressing the first idea for a novel and waiting for it to firm up into a proper rounded concept. (Some of the first notions for some of the novels appear here in *The Romancer*.) But even before this stage I have experienced a lifetime of reading and noting, either in the head or on the page. My reading matter can vary: great novels from the canon, novels contemporary to the times I am writing about; novels in the present day; comics; information pamphlets; documentary accounts; biographies; letters; diaries; newspapers; magazines; political pamphlets; history; aspects of sociology and psychology; songs and hymns; poems ancient and modern; myths and legends; local history pamphlets; paintings and photographs.

From all this material - consciously or unconsciously - emerge insights that are there at the service of any story I write. But what one absorbs from such material are not just facts, documentary truths or even creative insights. We have also absorbed the objective efficiency or personality of writers as it comes through their prose; the shape of the text on the page; the design of the book or pamphlet and the way it complements the messages in the writing.

Of course I have other ways of using material apart from notebooks. My visualisation of the world of the novel does not just involve writing in notebooks or on a screen. The information from the research is not just locked into notebooks or computer files for further retrieval, as it would be if I were writing an academic dissertation. For me, much of it is there in front of me on my work-room wall, developing eventually into a collation of paper and images in a somewhat messy collage.

This habit goes back to the earliest adult novels – it provides me with something to stare at as I am thinking or imagining.. What is up there? I will have tear-outs of contemporary dress and house style stuck alongside maps – drawn by me from imagination, or copied from contemporary sources. Sometimes I draw the character and scribble around them information about who and why they are.

When I was writing *An Englishwoman in France,* on my wall I had maps of contemporary and third century Agde, I had paper rubbings of a Greek Frieze I found in the courtyard, I had a glorious poster of the Ephebe, the Greek boy, I had images of esoteric objects from the local museum. I taped a fragment of a Roman amphorae beside the Ephebe, alongside photographs and postcards found there over several years.

I scrawl phrases and names from my research in oversize writing, alongside the names of all my characters; also my own wild drawing of these people. Things linger. (Up there on my wall I still have a native American dream-catcher– acquired in Colorado Springs when I was researching *Honesty's Daughter*.) As the chapters emerge from the novel I might print one off in very large print and stick it up on the wall alongside the pictorial stuff.

When I was writing *A Woman Scorned* - based on the true story of the alleged serial killer Mary Ann Cotton - I drew a whole street of houses across the length of the wall. This was the village where Mary Ann is alleged to have done the final deed for which she was hanged. In drawing houses I helped myself imagine the nineteenth-century street beneath the modern gentrified surface. I layered it with contemporaneous images and photographs to reinforce this feeling for me of being there, at that time. And it allowed me to sympathise and empathise with this woman. My friend and mentor Gillian Wales – who was instrumental in my writing this novel - also gave me a bonnet made in the present day but to an exact pattern of bonnet which Mary Ann would have worn. That, like the dream catcher, is still on the wall.

When I was writing *No Rest For The Wicked* – also inspired by Gillian - which is about a Theatre Group in the 1920s travelling from Paris to Sunderland, I was surrounded by theatre programmes, photos of theatrical performers, extracts from a diary of a woman who had witnessed the extraordinary funeral of Sarah Bernhardt. This scene opens that novel. I also had access to the logbook of a very famous theatre manager – Mr Jefferson, father of the actor Stan Laurel. It was Gillian who found this for me. I could go on.

This visualisation is not preparation *before* the writing. It goes on throughout the writing of the novel, until the wall is thick with inspiration and visual information. In this world of my study I can inhabit the world of the novel. I hear my characters speak. Paragraphs blossom in my head.

To be honest, I sometimes wonder if I'm inducing some kind of trance process more familiar to my Auntie Lily, the psychic.

The Observant Writer

In my writing workshops I am perpetually advising writers that, without the use of the senses, their hopes of producing clever, cunning, wild, or imaginative writing are dead in the water. My advice to writers is that the simplest way to force your senses to the front of your consciousness - instead of leaving them wallowing down there in the mud of instinct - is to *make lists* as you go about your writer's day. They are best written as a single word, or phrase. What are you *seeing*? (Precise colours, light on objects, shade obscuring objects). What can you *smell*? (Very potent lists, these…) What can you *hear*? (Non-human sounds, sounds of nature, fragments of dialogue) What does your *touch* tell you? (Let your fingers do the talking) What can you *taste?(Bitter, sweet, salty, spicy, soft as blancmange, hard as beef jerky)*. I tell them if they practise this very deliberately a few times, then it becomes part of their everyday discipline as a writer.

A workshop experience which we can do in any place – park or market, station or street – is to take out your notebooks and take fifteen steps, stop and make a single word note for each of your senses. Walk another fifteen steps and do the same. And another. Your senses will be sharpened and your notebook will be full of words, your brain full of ideas.

Later, these words and ideas can be woven into the greater prose enterprise of your novel, ensuring that the meaning is not skin deep.

Here, from my Agde Notebook, is a page of my observational notes:
Here in Agde any list for sight – colour, shape, light and shade - is easy to generate and would be a thousand words long. The sights – a brilliant sunset, pulsing light on the River Hérault, a rare cat slinking along the pavement, the sight of medieval Friars of the Sunday of Pentecost – are many and varied.

The list for smell is not always as easy. My list includes honeysuckle, jasmine, cigarette smoke (more than at home), bread, and that tomato-garlicky smell if you are in certain streets. But surprisingly there are not many cooking smells, when one considers how many good cafes there are here; almost no fish smells here in the town, although fish are caught and landed here and there are fish recipes on every menu.

This strange fact could be down to it being so warm. People often eat outside so perhaps the cooking smells are not so compressed and intensified by the cold air outside as they are in England. (This is mere speculation not science, but perhaps some scientist or food expert could enlighten me...)

But for me the strongest sensual memory of this place is sound. Perhaps because of the narrow streets or perhaps because of cultural style, it seems to me that these streets resound with voices – flirting, calling, bellowing, shouting, reprimanding, gossiping, laughing, crying, singing. At first, this may be a bit of an assault on prim ears from England, where emotion is sotto voce, swallowed, expressed behind closed doors, or otherwise under polite wraps.

I like the fact that in the streets loud voices ensure that families are within earshot, parents and children are aware of each others' presence. The love, the relationship, the blame, the praise, the reprimand, is a factor of mutual visibility. Children are most definitely not under wraps. Communication is everything. Here in the old city you sometimes witness it late at night. Young women keep their children with them when they have a drink, smoke and chat in the square then walk home through the streets, laughing and chatting and still calling their children to 'keep up, come here!' It may not be our way, but far from being intimidated the children seem confident and secure, right at the heart of their family, right at the heart of their town.

But voice is only one item on my sound list. There is the sound of birds: nightingales by the river, the modest echo of the oriole, the chirping swoops of the swifts around the houses, the offended cry of the seagulls displaced by these dawn and dusk intruders.

We also have the driving noise of the street-cleaning machine – specially designed for narrow streets; the scrape and haul of the large wheelie bins where we all put our black bags. This sometimes generates further noise in terms of shouting, when people try - illegally, it seems, to dump their building waste there (more voices!)

Inside the house there are the clicks and creaks of doors as metal latches close and open again – not in response to ghosts as one might wish, but to the wonderful eccentricities of spaces which were once alleyways, but are now rooms.

But for me the most significant sound in this town is the sound of two wheeled machines – bicycles, scooters and motor bikes making their way through the narrow roadways which are just the right scale for them. Girls in high heels and boys in flip flops ride them. I've seen young men doing wheelies on a small motorbike in the square. I had the thought that this modern day jousting has some echoes of medieval display, testing and daring as a kind of rite of passage.

Of course, normal sensible people would not particularly notice these sounds in this sunny, picturesque, historic town. But because I'm a writer and my ears are perpetually dialled to 'receive', for me the most evocative aural memory of this town could be a combination of the human voice on broadcast and the roar of 2cc engines.

These sounds are at the top of my list and both, I feel, will somehow make their way into present-day sequences of my novel.

And so they did…

Another aspect of observation and writing is my blog *A Life Twice Tasted*[3]. I have been writing a post there weekly, sometimes twice-weekly for eighteen months now. This is enjoyable writing, instant publication of short pieces about my writing life. I have found this a reflective, intense process, vaguely akin to writing a newspaper column. I think it is this new habit of writing short pieces - about feelings, reflections, observations, and anecdotes on the writing process, about the way I see the world, where I've been, what I've done – is what inspired me to write *The Romancer*. Perhaps this shows we must remember that for the act of writing as a learning and creative process to be most potent, it should be in some part pure delight, pure enjoyment.

Everything connects. Without *A Life Twice Tasted* there would have been no *Romancer*.

The Novel as Architecture

Like a building, the novel consists of a unique blend of art, form and function. The artistic element tends to dominate our discussions about writing. Poetry and short stories demand, as of right, exquisite and robust language, and distinctive forms. Their function in the wider world - literary and non-literary - makes an interesting discussion. I was recently talking to a doctoral student whose theme is, to paraphrase, *Is Poetry useful? Should it be useful?*

In contrast to these other literary art forms, I've learned that writing a novel also demands an instinct, a feeling for the architectural, large scale of such a piece of creative work. As in poetry and the short story the inspired, subtle art of appropriate use of language is a given. However, in my workshops I often remind people that a novel is not just a very, very, *very* long piece of 'creative writing' or short story. You do not create a novel by writing – however exquisitely - on and on and *on*.

There is a paradox here, of course. Good writing *is* about paring back, pruning and distilling your prose to the point of excellence. But writing a novel is also about stretches of prose, fluid rather than distilled, that take a long narrative forward, almost unnoticed by the reader. A good novel involves the integration of both of these forms of writing into a large scale construction which stands together as a whole – just as a complex building stands, its beauty in its function, its integrity dependent on its appropriate form.

And because novels are read by greater numbers of people across a wide range of tastes and tendencies, the balance between these aspects and the novel's function in society is worth thinking about. This does not make the novel more – or less – important than poetry or the short story. It just makes it different.

Novelists address the discipline of tackling the large scale of the novel in different ways. One prizewinning writer-friend writes on and on without pause until she has a whole heap of words which she then proceeds to slash, burn and distil to a much more spare novel, where every word is a bullet and the lines continue to simmer in the readers' minds weeks after they have put the book down.

Another writer friend says, with patent honesty, that she just sits down and it all pours out, almost perfectly formed. She claims that as she writes she doesn't plan or think where the writing is taking her. But perhaps she is disingenuous. I know her to have a disciplined, conceptual mind which does know where *it's* going, even if, on the surface, *she* doesn't feel aware of it.

Another writer will say his novel reflects his concern for society: it might contemplate the decay brought about by mendacious political values in modern Britain; or the alienated underclass; or the social consequences of greed. He says he brings his poetry, his prose, his characters and his creativity to the service of this idea, to get his message out. Yet another writer will create an elaborate future world which displays, in fiction, warnings about the state of the present day attitudes to global warming. These are writers with a valid, if didactic, mission. Some readers tell me they like to learn things from fiction rather than text books.

So, there is a distinctive difference between these writers and their approach to the function of novels. One school of thought sees the novel as a purely creative act which will resonate in readers' minds and allow them to find their own meaning, their own narrative. Others see novels as having a function: they can be useful; they can make unpalatable truths more palatable to the unwitting reader. When they are well written, such novels win prizes.

Some of us fall somewhere in between.

In some ways, 'useful' as they may be, the modern 'educative' novels remind me of Bunyan's *Pilgrim's Progress* and those improving Victorian chap-books written specially to educate the minds of the poor against the evils of drink and idleness and the need to be good. One sub-text of those books was to teach people to respect their betters.

Such books are part of the evolution of the novel form. There was a time when novels were a forbidden delight. Girls in some nineteenth century novels read novels in secret because their elders see them as corrupting influences on the innocent female mind. (A box within a box, as it were…) Some case studies of the sectioning of young women to asylums cited the reading of novels as a symptom of the newly invented sickness of *hysteria*. Novels were seen as a corrupting influence. While this seems laughable now, their perceived function in society then was clearly a matter of concern,

Of course, we *learn* a great deal from reading novels of all kinds. We imbibe facts and information, but often the lessons we learn are much more subliminal than that. We learn to empathise and sympathise, to see another point of view, to like the unlikeable, to analyse hypocrisy and dip into the subtle contrasts between good and bad people. We learn of a contract of private laughter and tears between the writer and the reader. Often we learn more about ourselves, about our own lives. We find we are not alone. Some letters in my post box confirm this. I have mentioned here in *The Romancer* the lady who wrote to me about how reading of Sylvie Sambuck's experiences in Singapore[4] - so like her own - made her cry for days for the first time since her own experiences.

I now notice that almost by accident themes appear in my novels that have a distinctively social or even political function. It's only in retrospect, in writing *The Romancer*, that I finally see that my novels do have underlying themes - the dignity and complexity of so-called ordinary people lumped under the reductive stereotype of *working class*; the peculiar nature of identity; the impact on the family of great events – acts of War and Civil War; industrial strikes; the creative dignity of labour; the restorative justice of education; the impulse to social mobility in the twentieth century; the heritage and unique silver lines of creativity that can run through families; imprisonment of the innocent and the guilty; the murderous depths of human nature.

But I have never set out in my stories. to 'educate' people about all this. It seems now to me that all these themes have emerged naturally within my stories, which are based on characters in the context of their time, on my own conscious and subconscious memory; and on my own close observation of life around me. The themes were never ever my starting points. They emerged because they are implicit in my view of the world.

But we need to remember that it's not necessary, not even creatively desirable, to set out on a novel with the intention to *teach* somebody something. It seems to me that any novel that emerges from such intentions can only be a very blunt instrument.

I think the key to understanding a novel, as well as writing one, is to view it as a piece of architecture. It should demonstrate a strong foundation in art and fact; a coherent skeleton structure. However experimental or original it purports to be, it needs to be predictable in certain ways. Using the metaphor of architecture, a door can be locked or open: an open door reveals interior spaces; corridors tend to lead somewhere; rooms have their different uses but contribute to the meaning of the whole building. Running through the walls and under the floors are invisible pipes and wires that help the building to function smoothly.

For a novel to do its work, it has to have just such a complex but coherent nature: the parts, secret and revealed, must contribute to the coherence and meaning of the whole.

This talk of architecture should not imply rigidity, blueprints or nailed-down planning. I think most writers have a plan from the start, if not a blueprint. For instance my plan for *A Dark Light Shining* was to explore the experience of an old lady I met who, in 1933 at the tender age of twenty one, travelled alone by train from her Durham pit village to Cannes in the South of France. In her true story she met two women: one, a bookmaker's wife, boarded the train in the Midlands, another - allegedly a *model* - boarded in London. In Cannes the three women – different ages and classes - stayed in very different establishments. Every morning they met in a café for hot chocolate. Ah! This novelist thought. The year that Hitler came to power! *What if? What if? What if...?*

Now *here* I knew I had a plan! *Here* I had a strong foundation for building a long novel about these – now imagined – people in those times. Planning from this stage onwards was, as it can always be, a wonderfully creative brainstorming experience – like a child listening at story time who, eyes bright with anticipation, keeps saying *what next? What next?*

As I've said, I know that many writers have differing and individual ways of viewing the architecture of their book. Each to his, or her, own. But it's always useful at some point to think in large terms when one is embarking on such a big project. This sense of architecture is what makes the writing of a novel a unique discipline.

To make such an apparently large task feasible you need see it as an exciting task, but also to break it down into parts, into bite-size pieces. I did this for my students when I was teaching a year's course for aspiring novelists (called *The Determined Butterfly*). For them I worked on a plan which I'd evolved from my own writing practices, called *Writing a Novel in Forty Days* (A Year in Real Time). This approach is outlined in full in *Appendix Two*. The plan worked for me in that year – I wrote the *Lavender House* - and several of those work-shoppers produced whole books in that time; others achieved a good body of work.

Although this is just one way to do it, perhaps The *Determine Butterfly* approach will work for other writers out there who want to develop their sense of the architectural scale of their writing.

Endings and Beginnings

It is very difficult to bring a novel to an end – by that time, the world I have created is full of real people and the events I have invented are remembered like memories. As well as this I have a sense of an audience out there who will feel the need for some resolution. A woman once came up to me and demanded why the bad preacher Edward Maichin had not received a proper come-uppance at the end of my novel *The Jagged Window*. Why had I let him get away? As we discussed Edward Maichin and his fate, I realised that, for both of us, Edward was a real person, as real as her neighbour, or my son.

It seems to me that an ending where everyone is happy ever after has fairy tale implausibility. Even then, when you think of it Cinderella's ugly sisters – possibly the more interesting characters in that tale – did not have a happy ending...

What this woman was implying was that Edward and all the other characters in *The Jagged Window* had life after the end of the novel. And I feel that for the novel to remain alive we have to have a sense of the lives going on. This was hard to achieve in *A Woman Scorned* as there, the alleged murderess Mary Ann Cotton is hanged in Durham Gaol. But Victoria Kilburn - my fictional character who is the eye of the reader and observes the downfall of Mary Ann - survives and thrives, her own life transformed.

Even so at the end of *A Woman Scorned* the Epilogue is a fragment from the letter from goal to Victoria from Mary Ann – the same letter that opens the novel is the Prologue. So, the end is the beginning and the beginning is the end. The architecture of that novel is a kind of eternal circle. It seems that Mary Ann continues to exist, speaking to us, as she does, from beyond the grave. (You might be interested to know that this novel, based on my reading of the evidence, challenges the received notion that this woman *was* the murderer she is alleged to be...)

Each novel has its own special means of coming to an end which will satisfy its own structural demands and imply life with all its challenges, going on for the people inhabiting the story. Increasingly as I write my novels I feel that each ending should imply a new beginning, a further story.

But as I said at the beginning of *The Romancer,* this book itself is a story of stories, a narrative of narratives. It has its own fictional drive. How can I bring this to an end? My own life goes on. My writing goes on. The fragments are still swirling in the drum of the Kaleidoscope. New fragments still join them. One shake and a new story is born.

I won't shake it again yet, though, as just now I'm half way through a novel about writers, called *The Art of Retreating.* I've been on - and have myself run - many writers' retreats and it has always struck me how interesting and odd writers are, when they are together. There is euphoria; there is depression; there is the meeting of minds; there is bitterness, jealousy and passion, There is even hot writing. These meetings are never less than dramatic in a very personal way. It was - as I have written earlier here - at a writer's retreat at Lumb Bank that the writer John McGahern restored for me my faith in myself as a writer and set me again on my path as a novelist.

In choosing the excerpts from this novel as the first Appendix for *The Romancer*, it occurs to me that, of all my novels, *The Art of Retreating* has a huge amount to say about the nature of writing and the nature of writers, so it is very appropriate to give you a taster here.

The Art of Retreating[5] is set in a house - the *Maison Bleu* – on the banks of the River Hérault in the Languedoc. This is near the city of Agde which is the location for my last novel *An Englishwoman in France.* You will see from the excerpt from this work in progress that *The Art of Retreating* has something of a comic edge to it: a new departure for me. In fact these two novels set in France signal a new direction for me, a direction which is energising and full of delight, ensuring as always that the act of writing is exciting, new, and full of promise. *The Romancer* itself – this book - is part of this new venture and has proved to be a journey of discovery, teaching me much more than I knew before I sat down to write it. It has been a labour of love.

Picture this: Our seasoned writer is sitting in her small study, dominated by a large, old school table set with the tools of her trade. On the wall in front of her is a dream-catcher that she bought in Colorado Springs; a poster of the Ephebe – a magnificent bronze of the very young Alexander the Great; there are three 1941 French fashion magazines, priced for unoccupied and occupied France; two postcards from Paris, same vintage.

Squashed into a corner is a small soft chair, with earphones looped over the back where she listens to music and her meditation tapes to calm her soul. The shelf beside her holds hundreds of notebooks: all her scribbling through the years. On the table are two baskets full of current work, printouts and a copy of Rose Tremain's The *Colour*. Also on the table is the fancy box in which she keeps the high powered radio recorder that she uses for her new radio programme, *The Writing Game*. She is enjoying this venture, recording both published and unpublished writers, and building an archive of Northern Writers. Her new dream is to get funding to publish an annual 'Northern Review of Books', modelled (with appropriate modesty) on the Paris Review of Books that publishes verbatim interviews with many great writers.

Beside her on the table is a higgledy piggledy pile of her own novels and collections. This is unusual. She doesn't always keep her own books so close, but she's just been using them to reflect on her life as a person and her life as a writer in this book she has called *The Romancer,* named after an term for a fantasiser, a story-teller.

Our writer is feeling pleased with her metaphor of the kaleidoscope. She breaks a resolution, shakes the kaleidescope again and starts to make a new list for the future:

- *Something set in modern New Zealand about a woman who goes there and transplants herself there from England*
- *Something set in Boston about a charismatic professor and a young prisoner*
- *Something set in Alnwick in 1960 - title 'The Room With The Adam Fireplace' a novel about this student - 18 going on twelve - living in a castle in Northumberland and*

discovering her real self - wrote half of this and abandoned it... worth going back to

· *Something set in Sunderland and Germany in the 1980s. Called 'Reconciliation'. A lecturer takes a group of her students to Sonnenberg - post war Centre of International Reconciliation - lifechanging experiences for all*

· *A Workshop Book - like 'The Romancer' only different - with lots of vivid tips and encouragement for new writers*

Our writer puts down her ink pen and sighs with something like happiness. That is the future taken care of. After all, a good ending is only a code for a new beginning.

Appendix One

Extract From

The Art of Retreating

Wendy Robertson

A comedy of manners set in a writers' retreat in the sun

... about Ruthie & Jonathan & Tegger:

Ruthie

The idea had been running around in my head like a scattered cat for years. It started just after the divorce - I didn't know whether I was on my ace or my apex, then, when I nearly bought this strange house up the valley - an ancient place inhabited in the seventeenth century by a Mr Foxe. You know - the one who wrote that old book about Martyrs? Maybe you don't.

I fell in love with this neat old house, sitting beside a stream in a mist that had settled in this slip of a valley like a persistent lodger. Looming beside it was a double-decker barn and my first thought was what great accommodation this would be for writers. In my mind I could see the barn lined with bookshelves and eager writers snuggling into comfortable chairs, scribbling. (I was called *Daydreamer* when I was small. And people smiled fondly).

Then, as I walked through the sprawling kitchen I imagined a circle of people all seated around a large dinner table, talking books and the terrible state of the publishing industry: charming people. Even charming *men*. (I'd not been very good so far, with charming *men*. The charming ones were mostly fugitive and the worthy ones were as charming as carps in a garage pool.)

I was just on the point of buying the Foxe house when I got cold feet. For one thing my bank manager was almost *too* keen. No risk for him, of course. If my venture failed he had my house in his pocket. Then one morning I woke up realising that the Foxe house, though mesmeric and historical, was too small for my purposes. I really needed a bigger place. And how could I think of risking the money, really, risk my small house, the only thing I rescued from the wreckage of my divorce from the second carp, father of my two children? They were now safely out of harm's way where he could neither elbow nor bore them to death.

The morning I abandoned the Foxe House, drenched with disappointment, drained of my dream, I crawled out of bed, left a message on the phone for my bank manager, and went to work. My job in those days was cold-calling for a kitchen building firm. You will say this must have been a dreary job and you'd be right. We worker- ants were watched like hawks. But the job had its good points: so many interesting people worked there on the phones – from unemployed graduates, to soldiers retired hurt, to housewives scratching extra money for their children. Our short compulsory breaks *every hour on the hour* were full of stories. So, if the work was the pits the company was great, inspiring characters and bizarre realities to texture my Daphne Byers novels.

Now I know you're wondering why a person like me was doing this kind of work. Well, the job didn't involve preparation; it didn't take much thinking about and the useful minimum wage kept me going from week to week, so I could get on with my writing, my true day job. Although my Daphne Byers detective series was selling moderately well at that point, the money - spewed out every few months or so as though from the hand of a parsimonious parent – never seemed quite reliable. And what if no new contract were forthcoming?

Well, it turned out that new contracts were forthcoming. As well as this, things began to change when I was sacked from selling kitchens. (My supervisor - a young, sour, controlling woman whose feet turned in - told me they were 'letting me go' because of my serial misdemeanours, which consisted of: chatting to customers about things other than houses; overstaying my comfort break; being found reading a Val MacDermid novel in the toilet, and flirting too openly with a soldier on crutches.)

I don't know whether this latter was because it offended her sensibilities that he was ten years younger than me, or the girl was jealous. The ex-soldier was handsome, after all. And a brave tragic figure. In vain did I protest to my stone-faced supervisor that I was researching 'soldiers' homecomings' for my new Daphne Byers novel. She knew better, of course. And of course she didn't believe I wrote novels anyway. She was something of a stranger to the bookshop and the library. And I have to say the Smiling Fairy was no friend of hers.

Anyway, all this made me think about the way I should supplement my Daphne Byers money so I could live a real life. That was when my mind went back to this idea of a writer's retreat. My qualifications for such a project were those I took to the smiling bank manager about the Foxe House: fifteen mildly successful novels under my belt and a reputation – indeed a degree of fame - for being a practical and pragmatic writing tutor. But I still worried about risking my own little house, so it would probably never come about.

But it did come about. It came about because of a woman called Aurelie LeBrun. After the drabness of the call centre and its interminable terminals I'd decided to treat myself to a little sunshine. I'd been going to France for years with and without boyfriends or carp husbands: Normandy, Brittany, Paris, and the Dordogne. Now - flying solo - I thought I'd dig deeper into France and try the Languedoc in the South West. This place, I read, that really doesn't see itself as France; it sees itself as something different. A bit like the North of England, I thought.

So it was on the plane from Bristol to Beziers that I met Aurelie Le Brun. Welded side by side in the crowded plane we fought over the ownership of the safety belt and collapsed into giggles.

As the plane taxis, charges, and then rises into the sky our giggles lead to conversation and I find that Aurelie is a businesswoman to the fingertips. The free way she talks about herself and asks me questions tells me she's not English even though her English is perfect. She tells me she's a buyer for superior English shops, shipping all kinds of goods from France to England. 'And you? What is it you do, Ruthie?' she says.

We finally dispose of the fact that I'm a writer and *she's never-heard-of-me-but-will-look-for-my-books-in-the-future*, when the flight attendant comes with her trolley.

We have tea and – at Aurelie's insistence – brandy. Then we sit back in our seats, assessing each other, as people do. Aurelie is tall with shining, upswept hair:

she's older than me, anything between forty and sixty years old. She's fine boned, with a delicate, intricate face. In her too-perfect English she begins to speak of her love for the English countryside and I find myself telling her about the Foxe house and my plan for writer's retreat. 'In the end,' I say. 'It didn't quite come off. Too risky.'

She listens carefully, her smooth brow furrowing slightly. 'So they stay in the house and just write their stories?' she says, clearly very puzzled. 'They just stay there and *write*?'

'Well,' I sit up very straight to defend my idea. 'They'll write and rest and talk. They might also go walking, swimming, canoeing. Even shopping. But there'll also be writing and reading, and a lot of talk about writing. These retreats are very good for giving your writing a boost. I was at one called Annamakerrig in Ireland, with writers and musicians. We wrote and the musicians composed and practised. And there was so much *talk!*' I smiled, remembering. 'One night we were still there at three in the morning, listening to two cellists playing against each other, like duelling banjos.'

Aurelie claps her hands, her heavy silver rings clashing. 'Bravo! How wonderful. You must do this, Ruthie! You must have your retreat!'

I find myself shrugging. 'I love my writing and I want to share that pleasure, that feeling. But …'

Now she's frowning again, her face concentrating. 'I have it!' her fluting voice penetrates the gruff hum of the plane and the trickle of conversation of the other travellers. 'I have it.'

I'm puzzled. 'You have *what*?'

'I have the house! I have a house which I am developing. It is one thing that my Serge and I do together. We take houses and make them good. So many poor old houses there, waiting for our gentle hands. You will have this house, Ruthie. You will have it for your retreats. For your writers and your writing....'

I'm still perplexed. 'So …'

'Your writers will retreat in my house, the *Maison Bleu*. You will make your fine retreat in my house. We will share the profits.'

'Profits? I don't know about profits.'

'Ruthie!' she says firmly. 'There will be profits.'

At the airport Aurelie waits while I check out and collect my baggage. As we walk through the big double doors, the bright white light and the dense lavender-scented warmth envelops me like a blessing. This is why I've been drawn so far south: to work, to drown my eyes in the light and warm my bones in the heat.

Aurelie hustles me across to a bright green Jeep where a small, round man is standing, his arms open wide. The two of them kiss and for a second they are the only people on the planet. She rescues herself from him and turns to introduce me. 'This is Serge, Ruthie. He is a terrible man but he is my husband and I must love him. Darling Serge, this is Ruthie. We are to give her a lift to her *pension*.'

Serge takes my hand and lets his lips hover over my knuckles. I feel surprise ripple through me. I thought Aurelie's husband would be a kind of mirror image of her - tall, elegant and cosmopolitan. But he's the opposite. He's five inches shorter than she is and a little rotund, with a gleaming hairless head and a generous, very black, moustache. His eyes, level with mine, twinkle. '*Bonjour,* Ruthie. Enchanting to meet you.'

'We must take Ruthie to her *pension* on the Rue de la Poissonnièrie,' Aurelie states, throwing her own Louis Vuitton bag into the back of the jeep before leaning down for my more modest luggage. 'She assures me it is very clean.'

Serge smiles, shrugs in my direction then jumps into the driving seat, I sit in the back and he turns to speak to me. 'Where Aurelie leads, Ruthie, we *all* follow.'

As we draw away into the traffic outside the airport they talk rapidly in French for a few minutes, obviously catching up. Her hand is on his knee. He nods and murmurs some agreement. Then she turns to me and says in English. 'My Serge has not heard of these retreats but he thinks it is a splendid idea, a thing of the future!   Serge is never wrong, are you darling?' She squeezes his knee again and I can see the back of his brown neck redden. I have a vision of the two of them bursting through the door of their house and making love on the floor without even bothering to undress.

Apart from murmuring Serge's name when we were introduced I've not uttered a word. Finally, 'Aurelie,' I say,' I don't think...'

She beams at me. 'It is nothing dear Ruthie. It is arranged! Tomorrow Serge must go to Pezenas to collect some carpets. And I will collect you at your *pension* at noon and we go to see our *Maison Bleu*, our house of retreat by our wonderful river.'

And that's it. She leaves me and my battered luggage at the door of my pension and leaps back into the jeep. She kisses Serge on the cheek and they roar away.

'Madame?' My landlady is standing behind me. She's about the same age as Aurelie but small and round and wearing a tunic apron. Truly, she's from another world. I follow her to a room at the top of the house. As the door clicks behind her I lean out of the open windows and look down sideways towards the port and the broad river beyond. Breathing in the warm intoxicating air laden with the smell of the sea and the ghosts of spices imported long ago, I wonder how I'm going to get out of this *Maison Bleu* fantasy, cooked up by Aurelie LeBrun. It won't be easy.

Jonathan Tye

Jonathan Tye was in the habit of saying that he'd been just another 'fat git teaching 'orrible kids' before Radnoy came on the scene. Radnoy was the raffish hero of *Radnoy's Quest*, his violently romantic novel of wartime Resistance in the Languedoc. His small, beautifully framed novel won him two national and one international prize with the added bonus of a rather bumptious award for the most unlikely love scene.

The rollercoaster started just at the time when his agent, the legendary Garfield Redknapp, had been telling him to '...*man up* – isn't that what they say now? You need to splash around a bit more blood and guts, mate.'

Educated at Eton and Oxford, Garfield liked to be one of the boys.

Then, on the very next day they learned that Mamie Hinton, judge of a major competition for novels with a foreign setting, had picked up *Radnoy's Quest at* an airport, read it on the plane and raved about it to anyone who would listen, citing its innocence, its erotically veiled sexuality, its urgent layers of meaning, its historical pulse.

Radnoy's Quest won her competition.

At that point critics called it in and put their own gloss on Mamie Hinton's praise. Punters started to bet on which actress would play the feisty heroine, which actor would fill the role of the flawed, ambiguous hero.

Jonathan's Mum, who took one heavy and one light daily newspaper, was delighted that her beloved son was praised in both newspapers. She held the heavy paper up towards him and his senses were filled with her hippy orange and musk scent under-laid by the garlicky tomato smell of the pizza they'd just had for dinner. 'See, Jon. This one says *it's in the tradition of Bridges of Madison County and the located novels of E Annie Proulx.*' She peered at Jonathan over her John Lennon glasses. 'Who's he? E Annie Proulx? Funny name, that.'

Jonathan reflected that with her sharp pointed features his mother had a look of John Lennon. In his later days, of course. 'She's a Canadian Writer,' he said, capitalising words as he often did with his mother.

She picked up the tabloid. 'This one says *Radnoy Reaps Rewards For*

Jonno.' Her voice was rising to its usual broken squeak. 'You must tell them to use your proper name, darling.'

In the end it was all he could do to prevent her from coming with him to The National Book Awards where he was sure to be honoured. She'd had a new version of her usual kaftan specially made by her friend Rainbow Stratton, who was allegedly a white witch. 'Rainbow made it so it will sweep the floor and hide my bad ankle,' she said.

Jonno told her, with all appearances of regret, that only Garfield and he himself had tickets. He omitted to mention that he would be escorting Tracey Masterson, the actress in line to play his heroine in the film of his book. She was rather an unpleasant young woman who picked her fingers but Garfield had insisted. 'All good publicity, mate.'

Jonathan told his mother she'd see it all better on television. 'Wear your kaftan and get your friends around, Ma. I'll fix you up with a crate of champagne.'

Garfield had even paid for Jonathan to be measured for a suit by his own Savile Row tailor, Ted, who would know– as Garfield put it – 'how to handle your *avoirdupois*, mate. Good with bulk is Ted. Can't do anything about the spectacular height, but he's good with bulk.' He waved away Jonathan's protestations. 'Down to me, Jonno! We'll put it against your royalties. Sales are shooting up.'

Pity about the height thing, thought Jonathan. The height had always been more of a problem than the weight.

Garfield was not too bothered about whether or not they won this one. The earlier prizes and the short-listing had seen the sales of *Radnoy's Quest* shoot up through the roof. The novel was mentioned on every television and radio programme that counted. Garfield of course, took credit for the novel. 'Didn't I say, mate, we needed to step into World War Two? With our boys in the Middle East now, modern war is *the* thing in fiction. Your Napoleon is lost in the mists of time, mate! Believe me.'

His publishers even re-issued Jonathan's earlier, modestly successful, novels that had been set in the France of Napoleon Bonaparte. These had only survived in terms of sales because they'd been recommended on some school curriculum booklists, much praised for their historical accuracy.

To give Garfield his due he'd really stuck with his author. Only in the darkest days at the end of his financial year did he reflect that his percentage of his author's earnings barely covered the restaurant bill when his author trekked down from his Northern fortress of a school to have lunch with Garfield and his editor, Naomi Colorado.

Naomi was certain it was *she* who suggested the creative move to World War Two, and – expert in Jonathan's style - said how very well he wrote about women. Perhaps, she told him, this time he should loosen his stays a little in that direction.

But Jonathan himself knew that it was entirely his own decision to write about wartime France. The April before he started the novel he'd been trudging the streets of the French city of Lyon when he came across some interesting letters in a bookshop. He was on his very welcome Easter vacation from the boarding school where he taught French and was housemaster to a gaggle of boys who loved rugby more than Alexandre Dumas. Jonathan, to be honest, didn't love his job. But the great thing about working at the school were the long vacations, when he repaired to France, set himself up in some cheap *auberge*, ate wonderful food, drank local wine and wrote his novels from notes he'd accumulated during the term.

This custom of flight had started at university when he realised that to go home to his mother for the long vacations was unthinkable. His sisters and his aunts would all be there. His mother's old hippy women friends would come at night, carrying their cards and their honey and bottles of home made wine. The *ouija* board would be out. That white witch Rainbow Stratton would cast her spells. Naomi was right. He *was* good at women. He knew them inside out. In his opinion women knew this and feared him. They compensated by calling him overweight and sluggish, offering him plans and pills that would make his slim and sylphlike. Even they didn't have the spell or the potion to bring him down to a reasonable six feet in height. The gaggle of women around his mother was probably the reason why he'd never married and why, at forty five, his image as a crusty academic bachelor was beginning to suit him.

But that was all in the past. *Radnor's Quest* was changing things. Women were now pulling him onto their radar. His fame and his filling coffers added glamour and mystery to his tall, stout frame. Strangely enough, Jonathan wasn't sure that he liked all these changes. He'd now begun to feel hemmed in on every side. He longed to get away from it all.

Perhaps it was this feeling that persuaded him to give in to Rainbow Stratton when she rang up to plead with him to help out her niece. 'Julie Stratton. She's an agent, you know. Have you come across her? No? She has all the famous crime writers, you know. One of her writers is that Ruthie Danson who writes these excellent mysteries. Seems that Ruthie Danson is organising some writer's retreats and Julie says she wants someone to help set them off with a bang. A celebrity! And of course we thought of you, dear. You're a very big bang these days. Jonathan, aren't you?' Her tone was very dry.

'We-ell…' He steeled himself to say no in the politest possible way. A crime writer! Like witches in a coven, crime writers.

She went on. 'It's in the Languedoc, Jon. Lovely area, but you know that don't you? Drenched in history. Ruthie met this woman who has rented her this small chateau right on the River Hérault. Looks beautiful on the photograph. Julie says it has a boat where you can row down to the city of Agde.' She paused. 'She tells me this place was the home of a group of German officers who occupied the house when the Vichy government crumbled. Those collaborators. So unfortunate.'

Rainbow must have cast one of her spells by the phone because now Jonathan was hooked. He reached for his diary. 'When did you say it was?'

Tegger

On Giro day, on the week of The Award, Tegger celebrated his win with his girlfriend Lolla, at the Black Bull, in their usual place on a street corner far enough away from their respective hostels.

'A thousand quid? Y...yum! ' Lolla smacked her pouting lips – not really a pretty sight. 'We can celebrate on that, Tegger!' For Lolla *celebrating* meant something serious up her nose or down her throat.

Tegger shook his head. 'No cash, Loll. Really, like. Says here the award covers the plane and this place on the river. Sun. Writing. Talking.' He frowned. 'Dunno whether I'll like that. Talking.'

Lolla pouted, her eyes gleaming through long blackened lashes that flapped against her fringe. 'Not fair, that, Teg. You should see some actual cash shouldn't yer? Won the competition didn't yer?' It was the first that Lolla had heard of Tegger's writing, when he won The Competition.

In his heart of hearts Tegger agreed with Lolla. He wondered if all the winners of the Room To Write Awards got their prize in vouchers and tickets. Or was it just those who lived in hostels for the lately dodgy? Maybe it was like clothes vouchers for the needy. He himself was *lately* dodgy rather than just dodgy because in the end drugs turned out to be not his bag. Even the thought of the gear had started to make him throw up and made him much more open to a *Dire Warning* from a guy called Cragan whom he met in the Black Bull.

Cragan – a strange, uneasy sort of man – had turned out to be some kind of a counsellor or doctor, and managed to get Tegger right off the gear. Over two months Cragan assured Tegger that he really didn't have an addictive personality. He'd just been having a really bad time in his life and was self-medicating. The two of them only ever met in the Black Bull, but somehow in those months Tegger got himself clean. He'd even shown Cragan some of his writing. This could only happen because there was trust between them. The last week they met Cragan brought him a pile of novels - battered paperbacks - and said he was going away to America, where he'd got this job in a psychiatric hospital.

Tegger never learned whether Cragan was a proper doctor and never saw him again. He read Cragan's books, though, line by line. And as he read them, it was as though he were in the Black Bull with Cragan, arguing the toss. The stories were full of people he recognised – people grafting on the streets, dreaming their lives away. There were even people like himself. This made Tegger write liked a lion, like he'd never written before.

Lolla was drawing lines in the steam on her cold glass. 'Can't see why you'd get money for a few pages of words,' she said. 'Not like grafting, or coins for playing your guitar at the station, or nothing.' Lolla called shoplifting – one of the necessities of her life – *grafting*.

'Just like grafting with a pencil, Lolla. Lying with intent.' he said, watching her finger move up and down the glass. Her nails were short and bitten but they gleamed with the residue of blood red polish.

'Whatever,' she said, now rubbing her finger up and down the long sleeve of her jumper.

'*Whatever*? Don't know that Cragan would see it like that.'

She grinned widely, and her face lit up in that way Tegger liked. 'Him? That old guy? Good thing he saw it like he did though, sending you that competition form all the way from America. An English competition! From America. The Internet rules!' She slurped off the last of her lager and looked at him expectantly.

He picked up her glass and took it to the bar. He liked Lolla. She was uncomplicated. She liked company and adored chattering away, mostly to or about herself. She didn't mind the odd sexual roll but was not really needy that way. She told him frankly when they first met that she could take it or leave it, sex. 'Mostly I think fucking's overrated,' she said firmly. He had the feeling she'd had some bad experiences in that department and left it at that.

She liked it when they talked about the movies they'd seen, and the funny guys in their separate hostels. Sometimes, just now and then they compared their experiences in the care system. Tegger was aware that neither of them told everything – the full truth - about that experience. Being in care you learned to keep your mouth shut about some things, to seal them safely away, even from yourself.

When one of them was flush - from a bit of casual building work on his part, or successful grafting on her part - they shared the bounty and had a big takeaway or bought a new DVD instead of a cheap knock-off. They watched it in the room at his hostel where there was more privacy. They didn't see each other every day. They lived in separate hostels and both of them liked their own company. This was convenient for Tegger who now, except for lager, had no desire to *use* anything. Lolla, on the other hand, sometimes really needed to get high and when this happened she went and got to that high place on her own or with other shadowy people she knew, who shared her pleasures.

Since he'd learned about the prize he'd read out bits of his writing to Lolla, to show her what it was about, what he was about. But she didn't really get it, 'It's too real, Teg. Nobody wants *real*! They want big, sexy cars and flash planes and raging shoot-ups. They want swimming pools and diamonds and personal cocktail bars, don't they?'

He'd hugged her, then, knowing she'd never really *get* him and what he was about. He knew he didn't need Lolla for his writing. He had all these stories lined up – locked up - in his head; about a picnic in the park and his mother's fair hair and her red tank top; about sitting on the stairs and listening to the scream and thump of rows; about crouching into the smallest shape as the blows rained down; about the views from the clinic window where he'd been sent quite often to be mended.

In that story he would write about the smoky froth threading through the city and the Angel of The North on the skyline. And there was a story in the smell and feel of the gym and the exulting testosterone-filled power of it all. And there were stories about his grandfather, who was a hero in the war and came back to a son who didn't recognise him. Then there was a story of a boy whose regimented experience in care had prepared him well for army life. This would have been wish-fulfilment for Tegger, who was very fit. But he was disappointed because he'd been turned down by the army, for some reason invisible to him. The day he got that letter was the day he'd started using cocaine.

Pop. Pop. Pop. Pop. With all these stories bubbling up in his head it was soothing to talk to Lolla about the need for a good lock on your hostel door and how *The Fantastic Mr Fox* was the film nobody should miss. And he didn't mind when she mocked him for lugging around a stack of pages and his little laptop in his backpack. The laptop was another thing that came through the post from Cragan. (He often wondered why it hadn't been nicked before it got to him at the hostel.)

He was very careful about his pages. Lolla said to him, 'The laptop, yes, Teg! Keep it safe. But who'd want those tatty pages? No resale value there. Is there?'

He didn't tell her he had this deep fear that the hostel would burn down and take his pages with it.

On Giro day, exactly four weeks after he got the Award, Tegger received a personal letter from Ruthie Danson who was leading this writing thing. '*Dear Edgar Conroy, I was delighted to know you achieved the Room To Write Award for my writer's retreat at the Maison Bleu. When I read your writing - so fresh and alive - I was in no doubt that I wanted to write alongside you and talk writing with you. You have a graceful, wild touch about your writing.*

I hope you will like this bit of the Languedoc. It's full of strange things – very foreign for us English – therefore somehow especially inspiring. I was wondering what your writing project would be while you were here? Or will you just be writing inspirationally? I know some people do. Each to their own, I say. It would be nice to know what books you're reading, what are your influences? I look forward to meeting you. Yours, Ruthie Danson.

She had slipped in a postcard picture of the house beside the river with her standing in front of the double doors. She was wearing a white shirt and jeans. Her hair was black, thick and short, springing from a point over her brow.

Lolla wasn't at the Black Bull that day, so he went on to the library and picked up a couple of novels by this Ruthie Danson. Only good manners, he thought, to read them before he went. He'd read *Radnor's Quest* by Jonathan Tye and quite rated it, although history wasn't his thing. But the fuzzy picture of the guy on the cover didn't tell you anything about the writer,

He made his way down to Lolla's hostel to be met by the warden who shook his head. 'You missed her,' he said, running his hand through his greasy hair. His face was grim.

'She gone out?' said Tegger quickly.

The man shook his head again. 'You might say that Teg.' His hard look softened. 'I know she's your mate. So I'm sorry. She OD'd. *Finito.*'

'What?' Tegger reached out to shake the man's arm hard. 'What are you saying?'

The man shook off the hand. 'Nothing to do with me, son! Happened down that Blue Street squat. Not here. Police were there. Bad gear, that's what the doc said.'

'She in hospital?' Tegger frowned, thinking of Lolla picking her fingers, of the smudges of lacquer on her fingernails.

'Yeah. The General. You can check there. But like I told you. She's OD'd, mate, *finito,*'

Tegger turned and ran.

It was a week before Tegger answered Ruthie Danson's letter. In the meantime he'd sat in on Lolla's inquest. The bad drugs were mentioned. It seemed the police were in pursuit of the dealer. The verdict was *Accidental Death.* Tegger thought it needed capitals. ACCIDENTAL DEATH. He used some of the money order from Room To Write (*'for incidental expenses'*) to contribute to Lolla's funeral and a simple plaque for the memorial wall at the crematorium. The modern oak benches of the chapel were filled with a crowd from both hostels, the hostel warden, and the barmaid from the Black Bull. Tegger thought Lolla would have been pleased about the crowd. She did like a party. And she'd have loved the coloured light streaming down through the glass of the windows onto the unkempt heads below.

Dear Ruthie Danson,

Thank you for your letter. I did not answer right away as a friend of mine died and there was a lot to do.

I will be working on – well, starting - a series of short stories all linked together somehow. About this girl. The book will be called 'People Don't Want Real.' It might even be a novel – longer than anything I've written before. Your retreat is my chance to do this. To start anyways. Books I've been reading lately have

been by Ian McEwan, Stephen King, Laurie Lee and Richard Dawkins.
Yours sincerely
Edgar Conroy

PS Most people call me Tegger.
PPS I hope to be able to pick up casual work while I'm there as the funeral bit
a hole in my money. Is there any casual work?

Ruthie tucked the boy's letter in the red box beside the others. His letter was curiously formal but it made her happy. It would be good to have this boy here at the *Maison Bleu*. He might just make all the difference to this gathering. And Serge might fit him up with some fetching and carrying. Couldn't have the boy with no money. That wouldn't do at all.

All she'd had from the American was a card with a green leprechaun on one side and a scrawled message on the other. *Delayed here in Ireland but hope to be with you on the 5th. Tom Ross.*

Appendix Two

Write A Novel in Forty Days (One year in real time).
The Determined Butterfly – Write A Novel in a Year

The method I use for writing my novels changes and evolves through the years. It's good to develop your method, it keeps your writing fresh. So I thought I'd tell you about a workshop I once ran, called *The Determined Butterfly* – about getting down to writing a novel in a year.

If you have reached this far in *The Romancer* and fancy a serious try at the writing game yourself you might be interested in what I offered them - a One Year Plan Based on a Forty Day Draft based on my writing of the novel *The Lavender House*.

Forty Day Plan For a Novel in A Year
Basic Principle – To keep the acts of planning and writing
creatively separate from the process of editing

This year I am going to try a method of writing a whole creative draft of a novel in Forty Days, later to be edited and refined into a publishable novel. I will go through this process myself and I encourage you to experiment alongside me and compare notes along the way.

Work freely by hand but those of you who work directly onto a machine will be able to adapt this method.

Length:
I know my novel will be 30 -50 chapters (many short!) and will be between 80 and 100 thousand words. You may have your own notion of length.

Preparation:

I see the novel as growing out of 40-50 scenes based on the embryonic plan already in my head, It is based on a place (London); a time (2006 and 1974), and a group of people (the inhabitants of two houses in a street in London). In the last few months with this idea burning in my head I have researched, photographed, mapped the place. I have brought these five or six unique people to life in my imagination.

Doing it!

I have briefed myself by writing single line scene ideas at the top of the first 10 pages in my notebook. (We have talked of the significance of notebooks…) These scenes are very loose, inspirational. I aim to surprise myself.

Next, I write the first scene quickly, freely, creatively on the right hand facing page, as per my own single scene-briefing at the top of the page. I can only write that scene on this page. (3 to 400 words) I cannot go over the page. This should be done in a single writing session of (for me) 1 to 2 hours. This counts as one day's work. I then think about what I've written but don't change or edit it at this point.

For my next writing session I work on the next scene-briefing in the way as outlined above. At this point this page exists on its own. It is not necessary that it continues from the previous page.

So, each day this free writing makes up my direct writing activity. Apart from that, I will be doing further reading and research, mapping and collaging on walls and in the back of my notebook I will be scribbling informed thoughts, comments, character names, location references which might be useful.

Every 10 days I will skim through the earlier pages, then make myself creative scene-briefings on the next ten pages and write these scenes on my pages as above.

This goes on in a cycle for forty days. By then I feel I will have the whole novel in essence. I have between 20 and 30 thousand words. This is not a plan or outline, it is the novel itself. It might need re-ordering in terms of sequence, and there may be a gap here and there. But the novel is there in essence.

Next I will put my novel in order. I will clear a few days where I can work continuously, put on my editor's hat, to work on this fundamental novel, as it is there - in scenes - in my notebook. I will read all the pages right through and brief myself on the left hand page about changes in the order of the scenes. I will star or highlight where the phases of high drama and quiet waters occur and how they are paced and spaced through the novel. I might shuffle around the order of sections or chapters to make the narrative work better.

Next, on a separate sheet (perhaps to put up on the wall) I will identify the true arc of the novel - the shape of it, the high and the low points, the way it moves forward etc. In this way I will explore the pace of the novel and see where and how it dips.

Then, reading again right through in detail, I will make notes on the left-hand page of the notebook, about further things that will enhance and develop each chapter and make it part of the whole. I will ask myself questions, deal with the unexpected. I can now do this because I know the whole of the novel.

I NOW HAVE MY FORTY DAY DRAFT. Hooray!!

Transcription: I imagine the transcription onto the machine might take a month's clear-water writing time. I will now transcribe and develop each scene from my notebook onto my computer, re-ordering the sequence as necessary, incorporating all the further knowledge and inspiration I've created with my forty day draft. Each 'scene' will expand into a chapter, or even two or three chapters. My five hundred words will evolve into a thousand or two thousand. Note that at this point, I am still *writing creatively*. I know and trust that my novel will be developing now in ways I had not foreseen.

I now have an 80 thousand word draft which I will print off.

Time taken: Around a month.

Edit: Again I retrieve my editor's hat and take some weeks to edit this hard copy attending to style, form, clarity and depth, to make it the best novel it can be. This is a good time to read it out loud to myself, or even onto tape, and ask myself questions. Does the language flow well? Is there music there? Is the prose working to make the narrative clear, the characters live? Are there connections between the chapters (or parts)? Can I identify themes that need a little reinforcement throughout the narrative? This is the time that I can make the small adjustments that will make my novel *cohere*. It is a good idea at this point to try to write a two hundred word cover blurb for your novel, showcasing it for your reader, clarifying it for yourself. It is also the time to clarify and make the title fit the story as it is now written. At this point I usually ask my regular first reader to take a look at the manuscript to see if it 'works'.

In this process it's important not to lose the freshness and creativity of those early page-drafts to protect its life and strength: no babies tumbling out with the bath-water at this point.

Now I will make another hard copy of the edited manuscript, as good as it can be.

Time Taken: This will take another month or so.

Finally I will put the completed manuscript away for a month, before taking it out again, re-reading it, making any necessary changes and sending it to my agent and my editor.

Time: One month

By my reckoning the whole thing will take about 135 actual writing days. These days will be scattered and clustered through a full year, in which my head - my conscious and my subconscious mind – are 'working on the novel'.

Of course my forty day plan is just one way to set about the architectural task of writing a novel - every writer has their own way of working. But *The Determined Butterfly* method really worked for me in that year of writing *The Lavender House*, as it worked for others in the group.

I was very excited about all this, because I just developed it as a neat example of one way of working – my method in a nutshell as it were. I am happy to say the method was adapted and adopted by writers who did indeed, write their novel in a year.

Perhaps it could work for you...

Appendix Three

Images and Books

Children's Novels
Theft (1972)

Lizza (1987)

The Real Life of Studs McGuire (1987)

French Leave (1988)

Sagas
Riches of The Earth (1992)

Under a Brighter Sky (1993)

Land of Your Possession (1994)

A Dark Light Shining (1995)

Kitty Rainbow (1996)

Honesty's Daughter (2003)

Historical Novels
Children of the Storm (1997)

A Thirsting Land (1998)

The Jagged Window (1999)

Where Hope Lives (2001)

My Dark Eyed Girl (2001)

The Long Journey Home (2002)

No Rest For the Wicked (2005)

An Englishwoman in France (2011)

Psychological
A Woman Scorned (2004)

Cruelty Games (1996)

The Lavender House (2007)

Self Made Woman (1999)

Social Dramas
Family Ties (2006)

Sandie Shaw and The Millionth

Marvell Cooker (2008)

The Woman Who Drew Buildings (2009)

The Art Of Retreating (2011)

Praise For Wendy's Novels

'A powerful writer'
Mail on Sunday

'Not only is Wendy Robertson a great storyteller,
she fills her books with characters with real depth'
Northern Echo

'Skilfully marries fact and fiction into an epic tale that has you
turning the pages at high speed to match the pace of this compelling story'
Sunderland Echo

'Wendy Robertson is a rare breed – a writer with an exquisite
gift for creating vivid, relatable female characters'
Scottish Daily Record

'A terrific read. A world on the cusp of change
and we experience it intimately'
Historical Novels Review

Wendy reflects on her life as a writer on her blog
www.lifetwicetasted.blogspot.com

For more information see website
www.wendyrobertson.com

Or contact agent Juliet Burton at
juliet.burton@virgin.net

Your Writer's Notes

Your Writer's Lists